9-10-06

Garis

I'm honored to share
our story with you. May
it bless your life

Sincerely

Doug Bassett

THE BARBER'S SONG

K. DOUGLAS
BASSETT
Ph.D.

CFI
SPRINGVILLE, UT

ISBN: 1-55517-848-0
v.1

Published by Cedar Fort, Inc.
925 N. Main Springville, Utah, 84663
www.cedarfort.com

Distributed by:

Jacket and book design by Nicole Williams
Cover design © 2005 by Lyle Mortimer

Printed in the United States of America
10 9 8 7 6 5 4 3 2 1

Printed on acid-free paper

DEDICATION

To Arlene

CONTENTS

ACKNOWLEDGMENTS

Shortly before I married Arlene Chapman, we were in one of those quiet conversations between two people in love. In my vanity, I was relating to her how I was going to make my place in the world. I painted a verbal picture designed to be quite impressive. As I added each new chapter to my conquering-hero story, I became hopeful of winning her undying respect and admiration. In fact, the longer I spoke, the more I got caught up in the marvelous "tower of goals" I was building.

At the end of my oration, I turned to my sweetheart and said, "Well, now that I've shared with you what I'm going to achieve, will you share with me your aspirations?"

There was a long pause. The silence hung in the air, waiting to be interrupted. It became painfully obvious that both of us were feeling uneasy. Then she spoke softly, almost embarrassed, "I hope to be obedient to God's commandments."

I hesitated for a moment because her response had really caught me off guard. The silence continued as I took inventory of my tower of goals and placed it next to her short statement. Comparing the two, mine began to look more like a tower of Babel. I recognized that the foundation of my aspirations had about as much humility as the "great and spacious building" spoken of in scripture (1 Nephi 8:26).

This was just one of the moments in my life when my words or deeds have made me play the role of the fool, but I wasn't foolish enough to let her get away. I have been grateful that throughout all of our time together, including during the events that I share in this volume, my wife has been true to the basic commitment of obedience to the commandments that she made long before we met. I am convinced that it is this which has brought us through the joys and trials that have been our life together.

A special thanks also goes to my son Preston for his help with chapter 11. His story titled "Soda Pop" is a major contribution to this book. I would also like to acknowledge the illustrations by my son Spencer that appear at the beginning of most chapters. I asked him to draw them from the perspective of a child. I feel that he achieved that difficult objective. I appreciate his contribution to the aesthetics of the book.

INTRODUCTION

The Prophet Joseph Smith said, "What is the object of our coming into existence, then dying and falling away, to be here no more? . . . It is a subject we ought to study more than any other. We ought to study it day and night. . . . If we have any claim on our Heavenly Father for anything, it is for knowledge on this important subject" (*History of The Church of Jesus Christ of Latter-day Saints,* ed. B. H. Roberts, 2d ed. rev., 7 vols. [Salt Lake City: The Church of Jesus Christ of Latter-day Saints, 1932–51], 1:50).

As our lives extend through the years of mortality, it is inevitable that each of us will lose someone close to us. It is the cycle of mortality we cannot escape. The longer we live, the more we will say good-bye, until it behooves others to bid farewell to us as we travel beyond this life.

This book is written first for those who have reached a point in their lives where they need answers or edification regarding their own mortality or the mortality of someone they love. People often speak of life and death as if these two concepts were mutually exclusive. This book is an attempt to bring together life and death—the latter being an extension of the former. More than just being connected, I believe they flow into each other.

The initial theme of this book is my perspective as a father during and after the life of one of our sons, who, because of his physical limitations, was forced to develop a view of himself that extended beyond his body. This eternal perspective gave his life greater meaning. I will share the things we taught him, as well as the things the Lord taught us. I will also include other family experiences and personal observations during and after the time period that was my son's life.

I am a teacher, and as such, I will focus on those experiences that are appropriate to share with the reader. This book is not a story that flows from day to day through a given period of time. It is not a eulogy, or even a biography, but a dialogue of observations and lessons learned, as well as doctrines shared.

I have not written in such a way that the reader can just have an emotional experience, though there may be some of that. I will, however, try to capitalize on the feelings created within the story line to answer the questions the reader may have. I have tried to anticipate doctrinal questions that might logically be asked at various points in the text. At these times, I refer the reader to the Appendix, where I quote the Brethren in an effort to educate, as well as to edify, the reader regarding those questions. I also include in the Appendix experiences that add to what I am trying to share in the text but that do not fit into the flow of the story line. The reader may wish to read the Appendix upon reaching the end of the book or look at each section of the Appendix as it is referred to within the text.

The late President Marion G. Romney is reported to have told a group of Brigham Young University religion instructors why he did not share more of his spiritual experiences by saying, "God does not trust blabbermouths." The older I become, the more important his counsel becomes to me. In this book I will share some spiritual, even sacred, experiences, all the while keeping President Romney's counsel in mind. I share these experiences not to captivate readers but to try to reach, comfort, and maybe even redirect readers who have faced similar trials of their own. The ultimate purpose of my story is to bear testimony of the Savior and my love for him. To this end, I will share that which would otherwise go unannounced.

1

A PERFECT SON

I have never liked haircuts. In fact, I don't know if I've ever had my hair trimmed more than a few times in my life by anyone outside my own family. I guess I just never liked the idea of a person taking something away from me and then making me pay for it. The exception was an elderly barber in American Fork, Utah, whom I met many years ago. I started going to him shortly before he retired, when I was just a young married man. By this time in his career his hands were shaky, and sometimes he would accidentally poke me in the side of the head with his scissors. (This may explain why his customers had dwindled to a precious few.) Still, I went faithfully, usually accompanied by at least one of my sons.

I brought my children with me because of something that occurred each time we went to his barbershop, which, oddly enough, had nothing to do with cutting hair. As this old gentleman trimmed our hair, he would sing the songs of his youth. Even though he didn't carry a tune much better than he cut hair, the manner in which he echoed his past touched my heart like a family reunion. He sang songs that I had never heard before or since about the land, the animals, his early years, his love for his wife, and other aspects of the life that was uniquely his. He wasn't just singing—he was remembering. The songs were road signs to help him find his way back. Occasionally as he would sing, he would weep ever so slightly and sometimes even chuckle, but never enough to interrupt his singing. These added expressions were a tender kind of accompaniment springing forth from his soul. They were somehow an appropriate addition to the lyrics.

As an added dimension, he would tell us what each song meant to him—I mean really meant to him, all the way down to his soul! His passion for life and the things he believed flowed like a stream from his heart to ours. When he did this, I never mentioned to him that he had shared a particular song or story before because I loved hearing him bear testimony of his life over and over again. There in that old barbershop, a seed was planted within me that now springs forth and blossoms into my own story.

As he sang his songs, the same continual thought came into my mind: "When I grow old, I want to feel as deeply about my life as he does about his. I don't ever want to forget the events that have touched and shaped me. But most of all, I always want to feel a passion toward life that supplies the kind of depth that gives joy and hope, even amidst adversity or pain." I didn't want to devalue my life with the passing of time by forgetting the intensity of life's moments. I have watched a few people gracefully endure to their last breath by remembering their lives in this manner. Without knowing it, they have taught me how to live as well as how to die.

My old barber friend was the one whose example made me begin paying attention and taking note of these things. While his seemingly ancient hands had seen steadier days and his walk was slow without a hint of youthful rhythm, he still was young in his heart. His laughter as well as his tears were those of a young man full of hope and love because he still retained the capacity to feel deeply about the simple things of life—past, present, and future. He had felt the pain and tragedies of life, which accompany anyone who has lived a long time. Yet, his was not the expression of regret or the remorse of things in the past left dangling but a celebration of life based on the gift of remembering. I loved him for this marvelous gift he gave me, even though he never knew what it meant to me. At the time, I had a feeling that he was filling up my reserve for the times ahead. Now, I know that is true.

I believe that is one of the purposes of staying close to the generations that precede us. For the day will come when that group has passed on to the other side, and suddenly those of us who were once young will be the ones who must sing our songs to the next generation. The barber thought he was sharing his music, but he was really helping build a bridge between me and my own aging, which echoed this thought: "Don't ever lose the passion of life, the capacity to feel so deeply about things that the sheer reminder of them can bring joy and tears."

I don't sing very well, so I will share the lyrics of my song on these pages. This book is a portion of my song, along with the hope that the reader may be encouraged to feel deeply in the most profitable ways about the events and people that matter most in life.

◆　　◆　　◆

In the Book of Mormon, Nephi desired to see the same vision of the tree of life that his father had seen. As a part of that revelation, he saw the death of many of his descendants due to their pride (1 Nephi 12:19). Following the vision, all the beauty and joy of the future were lost for a moment as Nephi said, "I considered that mine afflictions were great above all, because of the destruction of my people" (1 Nephi 15:5). Even with this weight to bear, Nephi gathered himself and his family and progressed toward his "promised land."

I am grateful the Lord has seen fit to bless me to see into the future somewhat selectively. When Arlene and I were married, we, as all couples do, started on our journey toward a "land" filled with "promise" but a land not without its opposition as well. How quickly the seasons of life change. A short time after we started our life as husband and wife, Arlene conceived our first child. Although we were stepping into a time that would give us great joy, I think we were fortunate not to have been able to see the challenges that were a part of our future. If this had been possible, we might have missed much happiness and growth in our efforts to sidestep the pain that lay ahead.

We were so excited about the impending arrival of our little gift from God. We studied hundreds of names to choose just the right one for our baby. We enrolled in a natural childbirth class and read as much literature as possible on how to care for a new baby. We spent many hours planning and dreaming about life with our child.

One afternoon, as Arlene was attending a luncheon, the conversation was directed toward a woman who had been trying to adopt a child for more than a year. She announced to the group that she had recently had an invitation from an adoption agency to accept an infant into her home. The news carried a great deal of excitement for those at the table. She interrupted their enthusiasm by saying, "We decided not to adopt the child." As everyone looked on, she attempted to explain herself: "The child was handicapped, and you don't invite problems like that into your home."

An uncomfortable silence followed as everyone at the table tried to digest her words. The topic was quickly changed to a more palatable subject.

As Arlene related this experience to me, my first reaction was one of shock and even judgment toward the lady. As I pondered further, I concluded that even though the words of this woman at the luncheon had been a bit coarse, there was something in them to which every parent could relate.

If it were possible as a part of the procreative process to design a child prior to birth, I'm confident that most parents would wish to make that child healthy, physically appealing, mentally sharp, and insightful. If parents could participate in this part of the creation process, would any of us bring our children into this world mentally or physically handicapped? Would we not wish our children to have all of the tools that would best ensure a long and happy life? Perhaps that was the thread of logic in the woman's ill-worded expression. We certainly would have wanted those tools for our own son.

◆　◆　◆

Boyd Marden Bassett was born in Redding, California, on February 7, 1975, weighing an even six pounds. What a thrill to have our *perfect* little son. But as the days progressed, we began to feel that perhaps our son was not so perfect. At first we didn't speak of it, as if by saying something we would create a prophecy of doom. However, the truth could not be avoided. His breathing was difficult, and he had a persistent cough. We were also concerned because he was not gaining weight.

We had him examined numerous times but always received the same comment: "Your son's symptoms are not uncommon for a baby. If he doesn't outgrow it, bring him in again for further tests." It was difficult to have confidence in this counsel as we sat up night after night with our little child. He seemed to be in a constant struggle.

A few weeks after Boyd was born, Arlene had the chance to travel with some friends to her home in Salt Lake City. With the doctor's permission, we felt this would be a good opportunity for Arlene to share our son with her family. Through the entire sixteen-hour journey from California to Utah, all Boyd did was sleep with a kind of unconsciousness that seemed deeper than rest. The depth of this sleep became manifest in his refusal to be fed. Arlene held him in her arms with a feeling that our little son needed medical help beyond her abilities.

Immediately after arriving in Salt Lake City, Boyd was admitted to Primary Children's Hospital. After a call from Arlene, I caught the first flight to Utah. While the doctors worked with Boyd, there seemed to be nothing for us to do but wait. Each day was filled with one test after another. Following a week of examinations, the doctor assigned to Boyd left town for a few days. We were asked to wait until he returned for the results of the tests. In our anxious hearts a few more days of waiting loomed ahead like an eternity. We wanted the results right away. Fortunately, they gave in to our wishes.

The task was thrust upon a student doctor who was extremely businesslike as he ushered us into a conference room. I'm sure his inexperience was the cause for his initial lack of tact. His manner made us very uneasy and expectant of the worst. Speaking somewhat like a professor lecturing a class of graduate students, he began, "Your son has a genetic disease known as cystic fibrosis." We had him repeat the name of the disease because we had never heard of it before.

Stopping his lecture just long enough to fulfill our request, he continued, "You and your wife, although not having cystic fibrosis, are carriers of the gene. Should you choose to have more children, each of them will have a 25 percent chance of having CF. The illness affects the glands, which causes problems in the lungs and in the digestion. The severity of the disease varies from patient to patient. Although a patient may not have a problem with both digestion and breathing, your son appears to have severe problems in both areas."

His textbook appraisal of Boyd left us speechless. After gathering our thoughts, we asked, "How long do you expect Boyd to live?"

Our question seemed to catch him off guard. To our surprise, his professorlike countenance changed to a look of sincere interest. For the first time, he was trying to discern our emotional needs. "I'm not sure, but I would think for your son about three years."

Arlene and I looked at each other, hoping that one of us might think of the right thing to say. It was as if we were sitting in a courtroom and had just heard the sentence of death passed on our son. But what was his crime? An appeal would have been useless; there was nothing left to say. We looked at each other with the confusion that stems from the difficult task of trying to emotionally deal with the unthinkable.

Sensing our need to be alone, the doctor put his hand on my shoulder for an instant and then walked toward the door. Hesitating for a moment, he turned toward us as if he wanted to add one more thing. The look in our eyes communicated that this was not the time, so he continued out the door. Arlene and I embraced without breaking the silence. There would be plenty of time to talk. At that moment we just needed to hold each other. As we slowly walked out of the room and down the hall, it was obvious by the tender looks on the nurses' faces that they were aware of Boyd's diagnosis and of the conversation that had just taken place. None of them spoke out loud, but even in their silence we could feel them reaching out. That feeling bore witness to the goodness and love of these professionals that would be a great support to us as time went on.

An example of this kind of love came the day Boyd was released from the hospital. Arlene was meeting with one of the women in the billing office at the hospital. This was a whole new world to us, and I'm sure it was obvious to her as she visited with my wife. In the midst of explaining the hospital charges to Arlene, she stopped and inquired, "Just what is your son's illness?"

Following Arlene's response, she slowly folded the file and said, "You will be having a lot of bills throughout his lifetime. You won't need to worry about this one."

With the stroke of a pen, she waived thousands of dollars in fees that Boyd's hospital stay had run up over the previous few days. We will be forever grateful to the wonderful people associated with Primary Children's Hospital in Salt Lake City for this marvelous act of charity.

In the days that followed, we pondered the path that we had just begun to travel. Somehow we were trying to find the way in which our path intersected with our Savior. The Book of Mormon states that Christ "will take upon him the pains and the sicknesses of his people. . . . He will take upon him their infirmities, . . . that he may know . . . how to succor his people according to their infirmities" (Alma 7:11–12).

Is it possible that Christ took more than just sin upon himself in Gethsemane? Did he take cystic fibrosis upon himself as well? (See Appendix, 160.) My wife and I were in a position where no one but a Savior could do for us what needed to be done. We were in this for the long haul and would need a much greater strength than our own to get by. Who would give us hope that we might be able to deal with this on a day-to-day basis? The answer for my wife and me was the same as it is for all of God's children. The answer is Christ. With the birth of our son, we had accepted the invitation to Gethsemane and to place our burden at his feet. It is only through trying to follow this invitation to "come unto me, all ye that labour and are heavy laden, and I will give you rest" that there was any hope for us to be able to deal with our situation (Matthew 11:28).

When I held our little son in my arms, knowing that he had been sentenced to three years of existence in a defective body and then death, I suffered anguish of soul. Arlene and I had not prepared ourselves to deal with this. In all of our conversations before marriage and the events of our first year as husband and wife, cystic fibrosis had never come up. Somewhere in my heart there seemed to have been an unwritten rule that children should mature, progress, and eventually bury their parents. The feelings that came to me when I realized that the order of things had been reversed are something I struggle to find words to describe. It was like the dazed shock people immediately feel when they have been in a car accident. They have witnessed it happen to other people every day in the newspaper or on television, and they have even slowed their cars down a bit on the freeway to view it as they passed by, but when it happens to them there is an emotional appeal that cries out, "This can't be happening to me!"

During the Civil War a *New York Times* reporter wrote, "A funeral next door . . . attracts your attention, but it does not enlist your sympathy. But it is very different when the hearse stops at your own door and the corpse is carried over your own threshold" (Ken Burns, et al., *The Civil War: An Illustrated History* [New York: Alfred A. Knopf, 1990], 161). I appreciated that sentiment with a fresh perspective.

I fasted and prayed for the Lord's direction in giving my son a priesthood blessing. As I laid my hands on his head, everything I desired made me anxious for his body to be made whole. But even in my zealous state, I had to admit I could feel no spiritual prompting in blessing him to recover from cystic fibrosis. I truly believed the Lord would inspire me to say the words that would heal my son. It did not happen.

How could this be? Hadn't the Savior taken cystic fibrosis upon himself in Gethsemane? Didn't he see my son in the garden? This confusion caused me almost as much difficulty as when I had discovered his illness! More than anything else,

I wanted to bless my son that he would be healed and live a long and productive life here in mortality. I also knew that just saying the words, even in a blessing, would not make it happen. I understood that the priesthood is not a license to play God but to speak in his behalf. As I gave the blessing, I was not prompted by the Spirit to say the words I wanted to say. At the time I could not understand the reason for this (see Appendix, 161).

In God's own time the miracles came but not in the way that I had expected or hoped. Gradually, over time, like a blanket unrolling, I came to a greater appreciation that there is a loving Father in Heaven who understands the destiny of each of his children. He also understands the pathway of challenges each will confront in order to reach that destiny (Acts 17:26; Ether 12:27; Deuteronomy 32:7–9; D&C 122:9; 138:53–56; Job 14:5). Without this insight, I could not hope to see the reason for this particular challenge in Boyd's life. As his life unfolded, I grew to understand it better.

2

THE ETERNAL NATURE OF THE BODY

How do you raise a child when he is not expected to
live more than a thimbleful of years? We worked hard
to discover the answer to this question. Obviously, if
the doctors were correct in their projections, such important
events as dating, scouting, or even baptism were not in the
mortal plan for our son.

In my own life, sports had been a major part of my
youth—especially baseball. Playing catch, hitting fly balls and
grounders, and watching or listening to baseball had all been
an important part of my relationship with my dad. Many of
the things he taught me about life, both in words and by
example, were tied to the rituals of the game of baseball. Even
to this day, my love for baseball and my love for my dad are
connected in ways I cannot define. Though he has been dead
for many years, I find that watching a major league baseball
game is sometimes like an emotional reunion with him. I

knew that my relationship with Boyd would not be the same as mine had been with my own father. Baseball was not to be an integral part of our union.

As a brand-new father, I cried out in my heart, "What do you teach a child who is not going to live long enough to play Little League?" The search proved to be a great blessing for our family.

A few days after Boyd was diagnosed, we took him back home to California. From the moment we learned he had cystic fibrosis, our daily routine was organized by necessity.

Immediately after we arose each morning, the first order of business was to head for the front room. This was where Boyd received his morning respiratory treatment. Located next to the couch was a small machine called a nebulizer, which sprayed a cool mist through a hose. The end of the hose was placed near Boyd's mouth for him to breathe. As he inhaled, the mist traveled into his lungs, which allowed excess mucus (caused by cystic fibrosis) to separate from the walls of his lungs.

After breathing the mist for twenty minutes, he would lie on a slanted board with his head at the lower end. Gravity could then help his lungs to expel the mucus. We aided the process by rhythmically patting him with cupped hands on the chest, back, and sides. We stopped periodically so he could cough up the mucus, which, if allowed to stay in his lungs, would prove hazardous to his breathing. The entire procedure lasted nearly an hour. We repeated this respiratory treatment each evening before bedtime. We added an afternoon treatment when we felt it was needed.

This activity was a rich blessing to our family. We used the time to read stories and scriptures. We also sang songs and listened to music during his treatments. We found this time to be valuable for family conversation as well. With this daily routine, it is not surprising that Boyd learned at an early age to love books. He had a hunger for learning that was seldom satisfied.

Arlene and I are convinced that this daily routine strengthened our family as much as any other activity. It's ironic that early in our marriage we owed a debt of gratitude to cystic fibrosis for bringing us together as a family each morning and evening.

Other than receiving respiratory treatments and swallowing a few enzyme pills before each meal to help him digest his food, Boyd led a normal life. He played with the neighbor children and rode his tricycle just like any other child.

Because of his digestion problem, his body appeared severely malnourished. His arms and legs were strikingly thin, and his belly was round and protruding. He looked similar to pictures of children from the deprived areas of the world. Along with this, Boyd had frequent coughing spells that could alarm someone who was not acquainted with his condition. The picture I have just painted of Boyd is not intended to be a specific description of children with cystic fibrosis. He had the disease to a severe degree. Many children with CF whom I have observed look much like other children their age. In fact, I have known people with this disease who have lived into their adult years before being diagnosed.

Perhaps because I grew up with sports being such an important part of my life, I developed an unconscious philosophy that I was only as good as my batting average—a kind of "good is as good performs" philosophy. The idea was that the better I performed on the field, the more worthy I was of happiness off the field. I'm sure this was not what my father intended.

Among the many flaws in this type of thinking is that it is founded entirely upon the body. Although it is not based upon the appearance of the body, it is still vanity in that it is based on a comparative performance of the body. This vanity then conspicuously projects itself as a visual manifestation of pride. President Ezra Taft Benson said, "Pride is essentially competitive in nature. . . . 'Once the element of competition has gone, pride has gone.' . . . Pride is ugly. It says, 'If you succeed, I am a failure'" ("Beware of Pride," *Ensign,* May 1989, 4, 6).

According to this definition, in order for me to succeed and earn the right to feel secure, someone else must fail. Feeling good about myself in this type of a competitive situation was always at someone else's expense and eventually my own as well.

Even if a person achieves success for a time, the body ages and cannot perform at an acceptable level. The fundamental problem here is that there is no spiritual tie to this sense of well-being. In this arena, self-worth must always travel from the outside in, rather than from the inside out. It is always tied to the scoreboard, with the things of the Spirit never being calculated into the equation. Happiness of this kind is seasonal at best.

In that kind of environment, Boyd had no chance of feeling good about himself because, physically, he couldn't compete. So how could we raise Boyd in such a way that he would not think less of himself just because he didn't have the same physical traits as other children his age? What changes would I need to make so that the jock mentality of my own life would not cast an imposing shadow upon my son's?

Understand that I am not against sports. Anyone who knows me understands that I am competitive to a fault. My concern was that I would not carry my own sports baggage into my relationship with our son to the point that he would feel that there was something wrong with him because he could not compete physically.

How could we strengthen him so that he wouldn't feel bad about himself when others pointed out his physical differences? Our faith in God and the gospel of Jesus Christ provided the answers to these questions.

The gospel teaches that the body and the spirit combine in mortality to form the soul of man (D&C 88:15). The Bible tells us that "all the sons of God shouted for joy" at the prospect of this union (Job 38:7). We wanted our son to celebrate this union as well.

Regarding this coming together of body and spirit, President David O. McKay said: "Man is a dual being. . . . Man has a natural body and a spiritual body. . . . Man's body, therefore, is but the tabernacle in which his spirit dwells. Too many—far too many—are prone to regard the body as the man" (*My Young Friends* [Salt Lake City: Bookcraft, 1973], 2–3). We felt that Boyd could fully appreciate his mortal body only by understanding it in connection with this "spirit" spoken of by President McKay.

Harmony between the body and the spirit is one of the major challenges we face here in mortality. Physical and spiritual fitness are not mutually exclusive but are connected as closely as the body and the spirit. It is hard to feel spiritually alive when the body is sick or out of control. At the same time, no matter how strong or fit the body appears to be, it is not whole unless it houses a spirit that is directing and disciplining its hopes and desires.

We wanted our son to grow into the knowledge that we best serve ourselves, as well as others, by understanding that when a disproportionate value is placed upon the body, vanity arises and the spirit suffers, and when the body eventually dies, what remains is a starved spirit separated from its mortal corpse. Truly, the reflection in the mirror is no place to gain a lasting self-image. The admiring eyes and opinions of others are seasonal, and the physical appearance that is approved of today is often unacceptable and rejected tomorrow. We wanted Boyd to understand the necessity not only of reaching a balance between the body and spirit but also of internalizing the total submission of the body to the spirit. To accomplish this, he had to accept himself as a "dual being," with the understanding that his spiritual self existed before his mortal body and would live on following the death of that mortal tabernacle.

We tried to develop our relationship with Boyd in such a way that he knew our love for him was not grounded solely upon his physical abilities. We taught him that Heavenly Father's love for his children was not based on the type of body each of us received as we entered this world (1 Samuel 16:7).

We taught him that while his body was a special gift from his Heavenly Father, there was an important part of him known as his spirit that lived inside his body. The way he treated his body had a definite effect on his spirit, but he should try to view his spirit and his body as being separate. We explained that before he came to live with mommy and daddy, he lived with his Heavenly Father as a spirit—without a body. In a sense, his ticket to come and live with us was when his spiritual self began to wear his body.

We explained that when the time came that he had experienced all that his Heavenly Father desired of him in this body, then he would ask Boyd's spirit to come back home to him once again, leaving behind his mortal body for a season. In time he would receive his body again in its perfected state, and he would then have it forever. This process is known as death and resurrection. When resurrected, his perfected body would not have cystic fibrosis or need shots, breathing treatments, or pills.

This is not a difficult concept for children to understand, especially when you relate this abstract concept to things they can see and touch. A simple object lesson that is often used to teach resurrection was helpful. I put my hand inside a glove and moved the fingers. Boyd agreed that the glove appeared to be alive. Then I slipped my hand out of the glove and dropped it to the floor. I asked Boyd, "Does the glove look like it's alive now?"

After he commented that the glove didn't show any signs of life, I asked, "What was giving life to the glove?" He responded with words to the effect that he understood that life for the glove was coming from my hand. I then explained to him that my hand within the glove represented his spirit and the glove represented his body. The separation of the body and the spirit is known as death.

I then placed the glove back on my hand and said, "This glove now represents the body we will receive from Heavenly Father when it is resurrected after this life."

I held Boyd up to the bathroom mirror and said, "Son, take a good look at your body. It looks different from your friends' bodies, doesn't it?" He agreed. "Each one of our bodies is different in one way or another. The size of our bodies, the color of our skin, and the color of our hair are ways in which they appear to be different. Your body is different from many of your friends because you have cystic fibrosis. Like the glove, your body is a perfect fit for you because you will learn the lessons in your body that Heavenly Father wants you to learn before he asks you to come home to him and eventually presents you with your body again in its resurrected state."

We wanted Boyd to understand that because of the differences in our bodies, some people might tease or say things that could hurt. He needed to recognize that "different" doesn't mean worse. It was important for him not to feel bad about himself, even though some people wouldn't understand that being bigger, stronger, or faster doesn't mean they are better people.

When Boyd understood this concept, it was easier for him not to base his entire worth on the way his body appealed to others, or upon its ability to perform in comparison to his peers. We wanted him to recognize that his self-image needn't revolve around the eyes and opinions of others but on the way he felt about himself and his Heavenly Father. The competitive words of comparison, such as biggest, strongest, and fastest, and so forth didn't carry the same importance for Boyd as they seemed to for many of his peers because he viewed these terms as being separate from his true self. This was not a result of our teaching alone; it seemed to be a part of his nature.

If these concepts were taught to all children when they are young, might they become a part of their nature as well? I am convinced that the earlier parents identify the eternal nature of a child's body, the easier it is for the child to interact with peers as the child progresses through its youth.

I had to make sure in my own mind that I was not adjusting the doctrines of Christ to fit my son's circumstances. The truth remains that everyone's body, no matter how much appeal it may attain for the sake of vanity alone, must return to the dust from whence it came. The value of the body springs not from the physical traits we inherit from our earthly parents but in accepting the body as a gift from God, to be developed and placed into submission to our spirits, which lived before and continue to live after the death of the mortal body (Mormon 6:21; Philippians 3:21). In doing this, we better prepare ourselves to inherit the body when it becomes perfected in the resurrection. Each of us must see ourselves first as spiritual beings for the simple reason that we were spirits before we were given this mortal tabernacle, and we will continue to be spirits after our earthly body dies. Only when the resurrected body is welded to the spirit are we truly in a position to discern the body and the spirit as being a complete reflection of each other.

Elder Neal A. Maxwell alluded to this concept as he spoke of his granddaughter Anna Josephine, "who was born without a left hand. The other day a conversation was overheard between Anna Jo, almost five, and her cousin Talmage, three. Talmage said reassuringly as they played together, 'Anna Jo, when you grow up you will have five fingers.' Anna Jo said, 'No, Talmage, when I grow up I won't have five fingers, but when I get to heaven I will have a hand'" ("Content with the Things Allotted unto Us," *Ensign,* May 2000, 74).

This kind of assurance was what we hoped to give our son. This teaching does not imply a lack of worth for the earthly body—on the contrary, it gives it an eternal perspective. As a religious instructor of Latter-day Saint youth, I have observed this as an area of conflict for many of our teenagers. For example, a girl may believe she is not a good person because she is too tall, or a boy may feel others won't accept him because he is too short. At the other extreme is the girl who feels her worth is based completely on the idea that her peers think she is beautiful or the boy who feels that without his athletic physique he wouldn't have a chance of being popular, and the list goes on.

I won't pretend to say that Boyd's life wasn't difficult at times and a lot of hard work for him, but understanding the eternal nature of his own body helped him immensely as he dealt with some of the conflicts in his life. Because we understood that Boyd's life would be short, there was a sense of urgency in the things we taught our son. The sad thing about all this is that if he had been born completely healthy, we might not have felt that same urgency to teach him these things. As I look at the young people I have served over the years, I get the feeling that many of them do not see themselves as dual (physical and spiritual) beings.

This brings to mind the analogy of the football coach and his staff who spend the week prior to a big game ironing their players' uniforms. I suppose the appearance of the team is important to a degree, but what about the more urgent preparations regarding the players' performance that needed to be considered for the upcoming game? Uniforms are important, but that's not really what football is all about. I feel that some of the problems with drugs, alcohol, and morality that engulf the physical lives of our youth might be avoided if they truly saw their bodies as an extension of their spirits. As parents, we may find it easy to get caught up in "ironing the uniforms" to be worn by the spirits God has placed in our care.

In this day and age it seems somewhat fashionable to speak of self-image. The world teaches that self-image is tied to the body and being productive in those things valued in a materialistic world. We hoped to expand Boyd's understanding beyond the physical realm and illustrate that true self-image has much less to do with how a person views himself than it does with how he views his Heavenly Father in relation to himself. "Having the image of God engraven upon your countenances" (Alma 5:19) is the only manner in which we can truly feel good about ourselves. In this regard, self-image becomes selfish unless it becomes a God-image that reflects upon our behavior. In a sense, our bodies become the classroom where life's most important lessons are learned. But our true self here in mortality is our spiritual self, simply because our mortal bodies will separate from us at death. It is important to point out that one of the keys that unlocks the gates of heaven is found in how we treat our own body, as well as the bodies of those around us.

This was the focus of our teaching with Boyd, but there was also another interesting sidelight that began to shine through in our life with our son. Because we recognized that our time with him was limited, we were forced to temper our view of the future with an appreciation of each precious moment we had with our little boy. Each day with our son was a reminder that today was all we had to be together.

Growing up in California, I didn't fully appreciate the summers because the winters weren't all that harsh. Summer days seemed to be sprinkled through the winter season very comfortably. But I have also lived much of my adult life in northern Utah, where I have enjoyed the summers more than ever because I recognize how preciously short they are. I have watched them approach with great anticipation and have viewed their departure not wanting to lose sight of a single warming ray from the summer's sun. I gained this appreciation because of the stark contrast in seasons. How comparatively short is the warmth of a Rocky Mountain summer, and how I have appreciated it so much more than in my youth, when many of the winter days in California allowed me to free myself from my winter coat and feel the hint of the summer sun on my back.

Such was the wide expanse of mental gymnastics thrust upon us because of our son's illness. Recognizing that the season of his staying with us here in mortality was so short, how could we not bask in the warmth of each moment, knowing full well that all too soon the seasons of our lives would change?

An essay by the late Robert Hastings expresses this concept well:

> Tucked away in our subconscious is an idyllic vision. We see ourselves on a long trip that spans the continent. We are traveling by train. Out the windows, we drink in the passing scene of cars on nearby highways, of children waving at a crossing, of cattle grazing on a distant hillside, of smoke pouring from a power plant, of row upon row of corn and wheat, of flatlands and valleys, of mountains and rolling hillsides, of city skylines and village halls.
>
> But uppermost in our minds is the final destination. On a certain day at a certain hour, we will pull into the station. Bands will be playing and flags waving. Once we get there, so many wonderful dreams will come true, and the pieces of our lives will fit together like a completed

jigsaw puzzle. How restlessly we pace the aisles, damning the minutes for loitering—waiting, waiting, waiting for the station.

"When we reach the station, that will be it!" we cry.

"When I'm 18."

"When I buy a new 450 SL Mercedes-Benz!"

"When I put the last kid through college."

"When I get a promotion!"

"When I reach the age of retirement, I shall live happily ever after!"

Sooner or later we must realize there is no station, no one place to arrive at once and for all. The true joy of life is the trip. The station is only a dream. It constantly outdistances us.

"Relish the moment" is a good motto, especially when coupled with Psalm 118:24: "This is the day which the Lord hath made; we will rejoice and be glad in it." It isn't the burdens of today that drive men mad. It is the regrets over yesterday and the fear of tomorrow. Regret and fear are twin thieves who rob us of today.

So stop pacing the aisles and counting the miles. Instead, climb more mountains, eat more ice cream, go barefoot more often, swim more rivers, watch more sunsets, laugh more, and cry less. Life must be lived as we go along. The station will come soon enough. (Robert J. Hastings, *A Penny's Worth of Minced Ham: Another Look at the Great Depression* [Carbondale, Ill.: Southern Illinois University Press, 1986], 90–91)

We wanted to enjoy our train ride with our son, knowing full well the station would "come soon enough."

3

LIFE IN THE
REAL WORLD

After staying in California for our first year of marriage, we moved to Provo, Utah, with the goal of completing three more years of schooling at Brigham Young University. One of the joys of Brigham Young University was attending church in a student ward. Even though the members of the ward came from many locations, we were all drawn together in a common bond as students.

Boyd's teacher in the Junior Sunday School was aware of his coughing spells and knew how to handle them in a comfortable way without causing undue stress for Boyd or the class. However, one Sunday when he was about three years old, a substitute teacher was brought in without our being able to instruct her concerning his illness. Apparently, after a few "hair-raising" coughing spells, she tucked Boyd under her arm like a football and with the urgency of a fullback looking for the end zone she hustled through the building trying to find his parents. When she finally found us, she let her emotions speak for her. "This child has a horrible cough! He should not be with the other children. He might cause the whole Junior Sunday School to get sick. He should be home in bed until he gets over it!"

Then she thrust Boyd into our arms like so much unwanted baggage and hurried back to her class. Although we were a bit frustrated, my wife and I tried not to be angry. Reaching for all the empathy we could find, we recognized that this sister's actions reflected the fact that she had been given no background about Boyd's circumstances. I have made enough of these kinds of mistakes in my own life to understand how she misjudged the circumstances. I'm confident that if we had been able to communicate with her prior to the class, her reaction to Boyd's coughing would have been different. I heard once that "each person makes a darn fool out of himself at least five minutes out of each day," and this was just her five minutes. If I didn't forgive her of these five minutes today, how could I expect forgiveness when my five minutes happened to arrive?

As she walked away, we were deeply concerned about the effect her words might have had on Boyd. We tried calmly but intently to visit with him to see what his feelings were regarding the incident. Boyd was a bright child, and we feared that if he had been listening to her words without understanding, he would have thought she meant that he should be home in bed until he died, without being with his friends in church. He was aware that his cough would not be extinguished until he left this mortal life, so obviously he could not stay home in bed until he overcame his cough.

As the three of us sat there in the foyer, we reviewed

the nature of his mortal body and how others might react at times without understanding all the facts. Even though some feelings were bruised and a few tears were shed, by reviewing with our son the concepts we had taught him about his body and his spirit, he was able to move forward with minimal difficulty. How much more challenging this experience would have been for Boyd had he not understood who he was in relation to his body and how people might respond when they didn't fully understand. We also found it important at this time and on other occasions to review our responsibility to forgive and not judge others when they make mistakes involving us (D&C 64:9–11; 1 Nephi 7:20–21; Matthew 6:14–15; 7:1–5; 18:21–35).

A child doesn't have to have cystic fibrosis to feel rejection, inadequacy, insecurity, or any of the possible emotions associated with such an experience. This is an event that any of us can expect to have at various times in our lives. My purpose in sharing this experience is to point out how the solution to hurt feelings was not in attacking or defending but in searching for understanding. How might Boyd have dealt with this situation had he not understood the eternal nature of his body and the fundamental doctrines of charity and forgiveness? Perhaps his basic disposition would have helped him get through those challenging times, but as his parents we could not abdicate our responsibility for teaching our child.

I will share another story, which bears testimony of this point. Our apartment complex surrounded a large grassy area that served as a playground for the children living there. The front room windows of all the apartments looked into this playground area, which created a kind of babysitting arena. One day Boyd was playfully wrestling on the lawn with a group of children. The fun came to an abrupt halt when a well-intentioned mother of one of the boys stormed into the group. Pulling her son from the pile of laughing youngsters, she scolded the children: "Don't play with Boyd like that! Don't you know he's sick?"

It is obvious what her intent was, but the method might not have been in the best interest of the very person she was trying to defend. She then emptied the playing field of all the children except Boyd. He was now safe but very alone and somewhat confused. As the parent of a child whose feelings had just been wounded, I might have had the natural reaction to attack or defend. Both of these strategies could backfire if not preceded by an understanding of the dynamics of the situation.

This understanding is simplified by viewing the experience from the perspective of a young child. How would a child think about his "best buddies" being scolded for playing with him the way normal boys play? Also, were these friends sent home because they were making a mistake by including Boyd in their fun? This was obviously not the intent of the woman who came to Boyd's defense; it was just the result of the experience from a child's perspective.

As we took the time to have our son identify his feelings, the answers once again came from the elements we had discussed. The circumstances were a little different from his conflict with the substitute Sunday School teacher, but the solution to both problems was the same. We asked Boyd how he viewed himself in relation to others as well as to his Heavenly Father. Therein was the key because if he thought he had less value than others because of his body, then it would only be logical for him to feel better than others if his body were bigger or performed better than did the bodies of his peers. Both of these mind-sets are based on a false premise.

Where did his sense of self-worth have its roots? We took the opportunity to reinforce a connection between him and his Heavenly Father, as opposed to the comparison between him and others. When the connection between a person and the Creator is made, then the need to rise above others becomes unnecessary. When that connection is present, it is natural that compassion and letting go of hurtful feelings will follow. This was true for Boyd at that particular moment, but it is also true for us if we are to travel well throughout our lives.

All children must experience rejection at times. Each one of us, young or old, must deal with circumstances profitably when we are treated by others in a way that could allow us to feel insecure about ourselves. Where, then, does the strength come from to deal with rejection? It comes from within. We must be spiritually rooted. In this way we can roll with the punches of life and move forward without bitterness, anger, or self-pity.

In this setting it might have been easy for Boyd to accept that being different was also not being good enough. This may be the same emotion felt by the teenager who works for months—even years—in the hopes of making the high school basketball team, only to discover that he or she has been cut from the team. This person may be left with the false assumption that "something is wrong with me as a person because my body does not perform as well as those who made the team." These are the times when individuals' understanding of the eternal nature of their body and who they are in relation to that body is put to the test.

A short time later Boyd and I sat together in the same grassy area enjoying the sunshine. My son was dressed in short pants and a T-shirt; suspenders rather than a belt held up his pants. The reason for this was that his digestion problem caused his belly to bloat just enough to make it challenging for a belt to keep his pants up. This is not unlike some of us middle-aged men, when we find that the muscle that was once located in our chest and shoulders has now become soft and fallen to our waistline—eliminating the usefulness of a belt and creating the necessity of suspenders. With his skinny arms and legs, along with his bloated belly, Boyd was built kind of like a pregnant pencil. With this appearance, his physical self was exposed to more than just the elements. At times the thoughtless verbal observations of others created some interesting challenges.

A husky youngster a few years older than Boyd marched up to us. Pointing at Boyd, he spoke to me. "Why is he so skinny?" He wasn't raising a question as much as it seemed he was making an accusation, as if being skinny was against the law in his home.

I have heard it said that "the pain we inflict on others is equal to the pain we feel inside ourselves." I believe this applies to the positive emotions such as joy and peace as well. This is also true of the negative emotions, which bring the kind of inner pain that cries out for some type of relief. Often our negative verbal expressions, then, become nonproductive attempts to relieve our own inner suffering. In this context, what we say about others often reveals more about ourselves than it does about those we are referring to. I sensed that this was the case with our young friend's comment regarding Boyd's body.

Maybe this child, who was more than a little overweight, had just left the breakfast table, where he had been reaching for a second or third bowl of cereal, only to be interrupted by the words of an older brother or sister. "Do you really think you need another bowl? If you have another bowl, you just might explode! You're too fat already."

With the painful feelings of rejection that would follow words like these, he may have gone for a walk and found someone like my son upon whom he could "inflict the pain which was equal to that which he felt inside himself" (see Appendix, 166).

Looking for a teaching moment, I asked our new friend to sit next to Boyd and me. I gently turned the tables by saying, "Before I respond to your question, let me ask you a question." Trying to keep my tone as sensitive as possible, I asked, "Does God love skinny people or chubby people the most?"

I could tell from the look in his eyes that this was the key to understanding his initial question about the shape of Boyd's body. Somehow, by himself or through the words of others, he had accepted a negative view of his own appearance. There are so many avenues in a child's world that can shape a mind-set like this. The elements that contribute to this dilemma can be connected to family, school, acquaintances, inappropriate music, or the simple act of watching unsupervised television.

He listened intently for the answer to my question. This young fellow, like all children and adults, was hungry to find out the worth of self.

I continued: "I can't tell you why Boyd is skinny or why you are chubby, but I can tell you that you are both important people. God loves all his children, no matter what they look like. The fact that you are here in your body is evidence of your Heavenly Father's love for you. One of the things that makes you and my son unique is that your bodies are different. Can you imagine what it would be like if everyone in the whole world looked exactly the same?"

He laughed, and from the perspective of children, Boyd, our new friend, and I talked about how life would not be as fun if everyone in the world looked exactly the same. Isn't it obvious that a lack of understanding in this area is at the root of many large-scale social problems such as racial prejudice? As time went on, our new friend seemed to accept Boyd to a greater degree. I hope that he became a little more comfortable with himself too.

This experience and those involving the well-intentioned mother and the Sunday School teacher are three isolated incidents that serve to illustrate that the challenge of self-worth Boyd faced was no different from that which any of us face as we grow and develop. Life was normal for Boyd because he felt normal from the inside out, and those who were close to him accepted his condition. If we had not taught him to mentally separate his spiritual self from his mortal body, we would have constantly been trying to shield him from the world to protect his feelings. In other words, we would have handicapped him without even knowing it.

If we were to visit the geriatric ward at almost any hospital, we would see the beauty queens and champion athletes of days gone by, now sentenced to the rest of their lives in defective bodies. We would be hard-pressed to convince those who still had their normal mental capacity that they are only as good as their aged bodies. As long as their minds are functioning properly, they are still beautiful champions who have accepted the reality that they are currently trapped inside an aging mortal cage. If they understand the gospel of Jesus Christ, they know that who they are is tied to the past and the future, as well as to the present.

Years ago I witnessed an example of this in a simple yet powerful way. An elderly lady, severely disfigured by numerous strokes, was approached by her grandson. He was holding a picture of her when she was a young woman. As he stood in front of this woman in the final chapter of her life, he exclaimed, "Grandma, you *were* so beautiful."

After he turned and ran back to place the picture on the ledge where he found it, she turned to me and said with a wink, "I'm still beautiful. He just can't see it."

Therein was the secret of her success! Somehow, back in the days when she was young and beautiful, she had been able to separate the positive expressions of others toward her physical attractiveness from the positive way she felt about herself on the inside. She understood that as her body aged and her physical beauty faded, she could still be beautiful because the foundation of her beauty came from the inside. Her reply to her grandson illustrated that she was truly beautiful through her entire life, from the inside out. When we recognize the source of our strength as spiritual, we will not be excessively pained or overly impressed when those around us judge us based solely upon our bodies, no matter what our age.

President Gordon B. Hinckley wrote:

> There is beauty in all peoples. I speak not of the beauty or the image that comes of lotions and creams, of pastes and packs, as seen in slick-paper magazines and on television. Whether the skin be fair or dark, the eyes

round or slanted, is absolutely irrelevant. I have seen beautiful people in every one of the scores of nations I have visited. Little children everywhere are beautiful. And so are the aged, whose wrinkled hands and faces speak of struggle and survival, of the virtues and values they have embraced. We wear on our faces the results of what we believe and how we behave, and such behavior is most evident in the eyes and on the faces of those who have lived many years. . . .

My wife and I have walked together through much of storm as well as sunshine. Today, neither of us stands as tall as we once did. For both of us, the rivets are getting a little loose and the solder is getting a little soft. As I looked at her across the table one evening recently, I noted the wrinkles in her face and hands. But are they less beautiful than before? No; in fact, they are more so. Those wrinkles have a beauty of their own, and inherent in their presence is something that speaks reassuringly of strength and integrity, and a love that runs more deeply and quietly than ever before. I am thankful for the beauty that comes with age and perspective and increased understanding. (*Standing for Something* [New York: Times Books, 2000], 93–95)

The counsel my beautiful wife received from her wise grandmother when Arlene was a young girl captures the spirit of President Hinckley's words: "Beauty is as beauty does." We realize the truth of these words when the physical prime of our lives becomes a fading memory, and we focus on the hopeful doctrine of the resurrected body.

We all have handicaps—some are just a little more visible than others. Doesn't each one of us feel handicapped in one way or another? Understanding this can free us from the chains of self-doubt, which come from performing the simple act of looking in the mirror and beholding our less-than-perfect reflection. The answer is not in running to the spa or gym for the mere sake of vanity but in building ourselves from the inside out. True physical fitness must begin with the spirit rather than using the appearance of the body to cover spiritual flaws rooted deep within the individual. The real self is not so much what we see when we look in the mirror as what we feel when we look inside ourselves.

By stating this, I am not implying that we should ignore the body or not strive to be in the best possible physical condition. On the contrary, I believe physical fitness is a necessary aid to spiritual fitness. However, we run into problems when vanity or the science of appearances is translated into the sole worth of the individual (see Appendix, 169).

So what did we teach our child who was expected to live only a few years in mortality? We weren't in a position to prepare him for Little League baseball, much less the skills of manhood, so we taught him the nature of his life in relation to his Heavenly Father. We taught him the principles that would prepare him to live with his Heavenly Father again.

I believe that children need to understand that their body is a wonderful, personal gift from their Heavenly Father—custom made by the Master. Within its less-than-perfect features and functions will be the divine lessons that will connect each child to our Father in Heaven. Can't all of us bear witness that life's greatest personal lessons have come not only through the body but also because of the very body we are wearing? Is this not perfect proof of the divine tutoring of our God through his great gift of a body, designed individually for each one of us?

The body, then, becomes a type of classroom in which

the Lord tutors us individually, giving us celestial lessons through the classroom we will wear from the moment we are born until the day we die. This individual tutoring is one of the reasons that the Lord can promise each us that we will not be tested more that we can withstand (1 Corinthians 10:13).

And what did Boyd teach us? He taught us to value the time with our children as if there were no tomorrow. By savoring each moment with him, we better prepared ourselves to live together as a family in the eternal world.

4

DIVINE OBJECTIVES
AND MORTAL BODIES

Elder Jeffrey R. Holland, one of the Lord's special witnesses, said: "I refer here . . . to those more personal *ministering angels* who are with us and around us. . . . Perhaps more of us could literally, or at least figuratively, behold the *angels around us*. . . . I believe we need to speak of and believe in and bear testimony of the *ministry of angels* more than we sometimes do. They constitute one of God's great methods of witnessing through the veil" ("'For a Wise Purpose,'" *Ensign,* January 1996, 16–17; emphasis added; see Appendix, 171).

Less than a year after we moved to Utah—when Boyd was just about a year old—my father had an experience that turned into an unexpected blessing for our family. Among other things, this experience helped us understand and accept Boyd's physical circumstances.

After having a major heart attack, Dad was placed in the intensive care unit at Mercy Hospital in Redding, California.

While lying in his hospital bed, he experienced another heart attack that caused his heart to stop beating. At this time my father's spirit departed his body. He related to me later that he stood in the room as a spirit for a few moments before he realized that the body lying just a few feet away was his own. For the length of time Dad's spirit was separated from his mortal tabernacle, his body was dead, though his spirit was very much alive.

He said that while in this condition, he was visited by a male spirit who related to him that he would not die at this time. The spirit indicated that, in a few moments, my father would return to his body and continue to live in mortality. He told Dad that he would be visited later and given instructions that he should share with my wife and me.

One of the things that made this first meeting with this angel so interesting for my father was that while he was conversing with this spirit person, he was also watching the doctor's frantic efforts to bring his body back to life. It was such an unusual experience for him to watch his body be administered shots, pounded on, and receive electrical jolts. When the conversation ended, my father said he slipped back into his body, and mortality continued on.

True to the instructions he had received, Dad was visited later and given the information that he was to share with Arlene and me. After the second visit with the heavenly messenger, my father summoned my mother and eldest brother, Bob, to his room. He told them that all was well, and he did not expect to die at that time. He didn't share anything more with them then, except that he had been visited by a heavenly messenger and had been told the time for his passing had not arrived (Acts 17:26; Deuteronomy 32:7–9; Ecclesiastes 3:2).

In rehearsing this experience later, Mom said, "Dad's face had a glow of joy that made it hard to believe he had just been through a severe heart attack."

Three months after Dad's heart attack, Arlene became pregnant with our second child. Each of my wife's pregnancies has brought us great joy, but with that joy has come a tremendous fear caused by the realization that because we both carry a recessive genetic trait, each child we bring into the world has a 25 percent chance of having cystic fibrosis. We had been counseled by some in the medical profession not to have more offspring. The decision for us to have more children came after much fasting and prayer, but this still did not keep us from fear and trembling.

When Arlene became pregnant with our second child, the nine months of pregnancy were a humbling time of fasting and prayer in behalf of our upcoming gift from God. When she was in the third month of her pregnancy, we decided to visit my family in California for Christmas. This trip came six months after my father's spiritual experience following his heart attack. He had been released from the hospital and resumed his normal life. It was during this visit that he revealed to us the message he had received from the spirit person who had appeared to him.

My father gave Arlene a priesthood blessing in which he said, "The messenger told me that you will bear a child who will be healthy." He also related other information for the benefit of our family. Following this blessing, he gave her a fatherly embrace.

The message delivered by the angel takes on greater significance when you consider that Dad received it three months before my wife even became pregnant! He knew she would bear a child who would be healthy even before she had conceived the child! If my earthly father knew this fact, then my Heavenly Father knew it as well. If God was aware of our second child's physical status before he was born, then were our elder son's circumstances known as well? (See Appendix, 175.)

I had to have faith that a loving Father in Heaven had established the "bounds of . . . habitation" for all his children in their best interest (Acts 17:26). Once again, I was reminded that there is a God in heaven who understands the needs of his children. After the blessing, our fears ceased concerning the welfare of our second child.

My parents had planned to come to Utah for the birth of the baby, but Dad had a relapse and was in the hospital himself at the time. He passed away almost a year after giving Arlene this wonderful blessing, having never met our second son here in mortality.

On July 9, 1977, Arlene and I received an exciting sixty-mile-per-hour police escort down University Avenue to the hospital in Provo. Arlene celebrated this wild ride by delivering Preston James Bassett twenty minutes after we arrived at the hospital. Weighing in at eight pounds, two ounces, this chubby little redhead won our hearts. True to the words of my father, Preston was blessed with sound health. Even in his infancy, he tried his best to keep up with his older brother. Because of this, it was common for Preston to have a bump or bruise on his head. He gained great pleasure from sucking the two middle fingers of his left hand. With these two fingers in his mouth, he looked like he was trying to whistle. We will always be grateful that the Lord let us know in advance that our second child would be healthy. It is amazing to consider that even though my eldest son was born with cystic fibrosis and my second son was born with a healthy body, both of "these children [would be] subjected to the very trials and experiences that Omniscient Wisdom knew [they] should have" (Bruce R. McConkie, *The Millennial Messiah: The Second Coming of the Son of Man* [Salt Lake City: Deseret Book, 1982], 660).

This experience, along with counsel from the Brethren (see Appendix, 176), does not support the doctrine of predestination. This false concept removes the agency of the individual and makes each of us mortal actors playing out a predetermined script. Such is not the plan of our Father in Heaven.

Many years ago I read a statistic that caused me to ponder our Heavenly Father's relationship with each of us before our birth here in mortality. It read something to the effect that on that particular year in the early 1980s there were 122 million live babies born into the world. At first the figure staggered me a bit. Then I did a few calculations and realized that if that statistic was accurate, then approximately four children were born somewhere in the world every second. In the time it takes you to read this sentence, at least twelve to fifteen children of God have taken their first breath here in mortality. Is it possible that God knows each of them? The answer is a resounding yes!

5

NOT TESTED BEYOND
OUR CAPACITIES

When Preston was a year old, we moved to American Fork, Utah. This meant an extra twenty miles a day for me to drive, but our new home had almost three more acres to live on. This made the extra travel each day well worth it.

While we were living in American Fork, Arlene became pregnant with our third child. Once again, the fasting and prayers began in behalf of our newest gift from God. How I missed the guidance and inspiration of my dad at this time!

Spencer Douglas Bassett joined our family on June 1, 1979. After our new baby's first breath, the doctor held Spencer up and exclaimed, "Say hello to your new baby boy; he looks healthy and strong!"

As Arlene and I looked at each other, we silently discerned each other's thoughts. We were happy the Lord had blessed us with another son, but we were also fighting back tears because we were concerned that he might have cystic fibrosis. Our experience with Boyd and other children with CF made it impossible for us to deny the possibility, and we were devastated. If true, we felt that it was our fault, and the feeling hung over us like a dark cloud. We had caused this to come upon our son. Perhaps we should have followed the counsel of the doctors who advised us not to have more children. Was our son the victim of our irresponsibility? All we could think was that we had brought another child into the world to endure intense physical pain.

As the doctor began to leave the room, I requested a visit with him. Even though I felt a little out of place, I said, "I feel very certain that our son has cystic fibrosis. Could you please place him in the intensive care unit?"

"Nonsense," replied the doctor. "CF can't even be diagnosed without a sweat test. The baby has to be a month old before that test can be performed."

I continued to plead: "Please believe me, he has cystic fibrosis. He must be placed in intensive care. I believe the delay could be serious."

Placing his hand on my arm, he looked at me and tried compassionately to get his point across. "Your child is healthy—trust me." He then walked away.

I was not angry. I could understand his position. After all, who was I to be counseling a professional? However, I continued to pursue the issue. I stood outside a room in the pediatric ward, watching a nurse wash Spencer and prepare him to be placed in the nursery with the other babies.

When she finished her task and began moving toward another room, I gained an audience with her. I said, "I know this sounds crazy, but I feel quite sure that my son has some health problems. We have an older son with cystic fibrosis, and I feel this boy has the same illness."

Her reaction was similar to the doctor's. Her smile gave me the feeling that she was thinking to herself, "Here we go again, another overzealous father." She then said, "We'll keep an eye on him, and we will let you know if anything develops. Why don't you have a visit with your wife and then go home? Everything will be fine here."

I decided to follow her advice. It seemed to be the only thing left to do. That night was filled with personal anguish. I thought the morning was never going to come. When the sun finally arrived, I left Boyd (four years old) and Preston (two years old) with my mother, who was visiting from California, and sped to the hospital.

I went immediately to the room where I had last seen Spencer. The room had a number of clear boxes on wheels, each containing a baby. These boxes, which were open at the top, were lined up like cars in a small used car lot. With a quick inspection, I could see my son was not among them. The little bed with his name on it had vanished as well. With my heart slowly sinking, I continued down the hallway to the intensive care unit.

As I surveyed the room, I realized that this area was much different from the room with the healthy babies. The obvious difference was that this section was filled with machines and monitors, with only a few clear boxes. Another distinctive feature was that, unlike the half-boxes in the room I had just left, many of these clear boxes were completely enclosed. My eyes caught sight of one of these containers. Fastened to the outside was a clipboard with some writing in bold, black felt-tip pen. Like a solemn announcement, it read: "Bassett

Baby." Inside this sterile crib was a baby who was connected to so many wires and tubes that he looked like a puppet. With somber resolve, I recognized him as my child.

I leaned against the window separating the intensive care room from the hall. The feeling of being dazed and confused engulfed me like a cloud. I felt like I had been in some kind of emotional boxing match in which I was reeling from a major blow. A sense of spiritual suffocation gripped me from deep inside. I felt as if the Lord had let me, my wife, and my baby down. I could not escape the feeling that we had been forgotten, as well as forsaken, by our God. My feelings for my Heavenly Father—my hope, as well as my faith—were suddenly being challenged by an overwhelming sense of frustration.

I understood with a new perspective the words of Alma when he said, "Oh, thought I, that I could be banished and become extinct both soul and body" (Alma 36:15). The feeling of being completely lost shrouded my very being and penetrated to the deepest part of my soul. In that instant I understood depression as I never had before. My will to endure had been replaced, for the moment, by a tremendous urge to escape. Perhaps it is not possible to fully appreciate the power of hope until it no longer is a part of us. I know that was true for me.

Just then, our doctor came into the hall. I'm sure that he felt my emotions when my eyes—penetrating, desperately searching for someone to blame—focused on him. He did not appear as confident as the day before when he said, "Your son has a block in his intestines." My frustration surfaced, and I spoke abruptly. "This is caused by cystic fibrosis, isn't it?" My words were a challenge as much as a question.

"That is possible. We are going to attempt to get the block to pass by giving him a series of radiological enemas. If this does not work, then we will be forced to perform surgery. We may have to remove a portion of his intestine."

With no emotion, I nodded my head, turned, and walked away with no real destination in mind. The overwhelming burden of present events had left me empty. The weight of my own body felt like a piano on my back. Little did I know that this good man would then travel up to my wife's room, lift her from the chair on which she had been sitting dejectedly, hold her in his arms, and comfort and weep with her.

In my own despair, I came to an elevator and, without thinking, pressed the basement-floor button. Like a man drunken in his thoughts, I wandered through an empty basement hallway. I came to a small room and, immediately after flipping on the light switch, sank to the floor. I felt betrayed, and my faith, which had always been a strength to me, was severely wavering. I thought of my wife upstairs, once again having to watch the other mothers receive their babies and witness their excitement in contrast to her tremendous sadness. How could she not envy them? This woman, who had been obedient to the commandments all her life, was now going to carry a weight that she seemed not to deserve! I thought of the scripture that states, "Wickedness never was happiness" (Alma 41:10). If wickedness brings sadness, where was the wickedness on her part? Where was the reward for her obedience?

I thought of her seeing her child suffering, and of her aching for having been a part of it. She would even have to endure the comments of those who would question her having more children even though she understood the possibility of CF. How many times would we ask ourselves that same question?

My emotions were such that I didn't even kneel as I verbally poured out my frustrations toward heaven. "How are we ever going to care for another child with CF? I work full time, I go to school full time, and I catch up on my sleep on the weekends. Why has this baby been sent to us now?" Like a demanding child, I exclaimed, "I just can't see how a loving Father in Heaven could do this to a child. I just don't understand you!"

No more words came as I sank silently to the floor, defeated by my circumstances. In the midst of my anxiety, a warmth, which encompassed me both spiritually and physically, suddenly overwhelmed me. I was immersed in spirit from the top of my head to the soles of my feet. I was so engulfed by this moment that I was unaware of the passing of time. In the midst of this event, words came into my mind, which were placed there by that same spirit: "Your child is my child too, and neither you nor he will be tested more than you are able to bear."

It was a total immersion in the "love of God," which Nephi spoke of as "the most desirable above all things" (1 Nephi 11:21–23). I knew that Nephi was right. I felt cleansed and comforted down to my soul. My tears of bitterness were replaced with tears of joy, as I thanked my Father in Heaven for his loving care. It was surprising that such deep negative feelings could be replaced so quickly with such an overwhelming sense of peace and joy. I knew that this was a spiritual gift from my Heavenly Father. I was overwhelmed by his goodness.

As I stood up, I realized that my prayer had not been

answered in the way I had expected. I still didn't know why Spencer had cystic fibrosis, but I was sure that God knew, and that was enough. I knew that all would be well according to his will, and I placed full trust in that knowledge. Spencer was his child too, and he would help us care for him. The affirmation that we would not be tested beyond our capacity to withstand was a great comfort to me (1 Corinthians 10:13; Appendix, 177).

From my experience and from studying the testimonies of the Brethren, I am convinced that the body Spencer received was not an accident to God. Spencer was aware of the circumstances he would have physically before he even came to this earth. Who we are physically is not a game of chance to the Father who created us all.

I walked out of that room physically exhausted because of what I had experienced. At the same time, I was relieved and ready to face life. I had no particular plan in mind, but I felt with God's help all would be well. Scared of my own inability and afraid of the future, I was willing to be "led by the Spirit, not knowing beforehand the things which I should do" (1 Nephi 4:6).

A short time later, I went upstairs to the intensive care room where Arlene was waiting. I laid my hands on our new baby's head to give him a priesthood blessing. My feelings were much different in this blessing from those I had when I had administered to Boyd as a baby. Although I was not inspired to refer to his cystic fibrosis, I was prompted to promise him that he would not have to have surgery. In the blessing, I reviewed the feelings I had just received from my Heavenly Father.

Shortly after the blessing, Spencer was transferred to

Primary Children's Hospital in Salt Lake City. The doctors wanted one last attempt to clear his blocked intestine prior to surgery. Spencer was given another series of enemas. True to the blessing, his intestinal blockage dislodged, and he was able to avoid surgery.

Boyd and Preston were allowed a visit with their new baby brother in the hospital. They scrubbed their hands and wore special gowns just like the doctors. Boyd held Spencer in the rocking chair, and with a feeling of joyous kinship announced, "He has CF too!"

A few days later we were able to bring Spencer home from the hospital. On the way, Boyd said, "We're sure lucky to have Spencer."

Arlene and I could not have said it better (see Appendix, 178).

6

JESUS' CAR

An experience we had when Boyd was almost four years old illustrates that it is never too early to help a child become spiritually grounded. It has been well documented that much of how an adult sees himself in relation to the world occurs in the first five formative years of life.

There was no question in Boyd's mind that the most valuable possession in our home was a toy car that was small enough to fit in the palm of my hand. It was not referred to as a station wagon or the little blue car—it was simply known as "Boyd's car." Day after day the tiny car could be found at his side. When he stopped for a meal, the car would rest beside his plate. For the rest of the family, the table setting would involve the traditional knife, fork, and spoon, but for our son, the order of utensils was as follows: knife, fork, spoon, and "Boyd's car." When he slept he shared his pillow with the car. Rolling over in the night and bumping his head against a fender was not a deterrent in his kinship with "Boyd's car." When he bathed, the bathtub was magically transformed into a car wash for his four-wheeled friend. To our little son, the car was more than a playmate—it was Boyd's confidant and companion.

Then one day, life with "Boyd's car" hit a major bump in the road—he lost his toy! Frantically, he searched here and there but to no avail; the car seemed to be gone forever.

At this point in Boyd's life, we were looking for every opportunity to strengthen his relationship with his Heavenly Father so that when his time to die came (D&C 64:32), he would not be fearful of passing into the next chapter of his eternal progression. I cannot explain why—I'm not sure I understand myself—but I was not as afraid of his death as I was about not preparing him properly to die. Perhaps an analogy can best express my feelings. Because Boyd was a boy, let us assume that the child in this analogy is also a boy.

When parents leave a small child at a babysitter's house, it is not unusual for the child to cry. Parents might assure their offspring that they won't be gone too long. At this tender age a child does not understand what "long" is, so he continues to cry. After the assurances of the babysitter, the parents close the front door behind them, expecting that the child will stop crying soon and begin to occupy himself with something in his new surroundings.

With this hope in mind, Mom and Dad climb into the car and start the engine. As they back out of the driveway, they glance in the direction of the house, only to see their child pressed frantically against the front room window, his face disfigured against the glass in an attempt to reach them. Obviously, the child has not warmed up to his new environment. Trusting in the babysitter, the parents reassure each other that all will be well and decide to call during the intermission of the movie they will be attending. Having faith in that thought, they continue out of the driveway and down the road. They call at intermission and are comforted by the fact that the child has bonded with his new surroundings—at least long enough for them to finish the movie.

My fear was that when it came time for Boyd to move from our home back to his Heavenly Father, he might approach his heavenly home with the same fear and trembling as the child in my analogy did toward the babysitter's residence. I understood that there was no second chance in getting this task done properly. Unlike the analogy of the babysitter, I wouldn't get to "call at intermission" to see how he was doing. I felt so inadequate as a parent that I feared he might view his Heavenly Father as a babysitter.

To make matters more challenging, the loss of "Boyd's car" occurred during finals week of my senior year in college. To say the least, my mind was focused on other things. Even so, I saw the lost car as an opportunity to reinforce the connection between our child and his Heavenly Father.

Though the situation was a little unusual, I felt good about promising Boyd that if he prayed each morning and night for direction, Heavenly Father and Jesus would help him find his car. I rationalized that if Christ was mindful of all the "sparrows" and the "lilies" (Matthew 10:29; 6:28), then he just might have an eye on "Boyd's car."

The first few days of our prayer project went great. Boyd's faith never wavered, but as the days passed, mine began to tremble. My son didn't lose faith in my words, but I did. I began to question my right to make such a promise to him.

"After all," I thought, "that car is probably smashed as flat as a pancake under a truck somewhere, and it's going to take a minor resurrection to bring it back."

When my thoughts turned to other things, Boyd continued his prayer project in earnest. At first we prayed together, but when my faith started to waver, Boyd continued to pray by himself. I hoped the limited attention span of youth would catch up with Boyd and he would become interested in something else and forget about his favorite toy car.

One evening when I returned home from a particularly tiring day at school, Arlene met me at the door and announced, "Boyd has something to show you!"

Boyd ran up and exclaimed, "Daddy, look!" Into his hand the prodigal car had returned. I got down on one knee next to Boyd to share in his joy. "Son, you found your car!"

He stepped back, a little surprised and somewhat confused. When I inquired what was the matter, he confided, "Don't you remember, Daddy? Heavenly Father and Jesus found the car."

In his eyes I could see what the Savior meant when he admonished the disciples to "become as little children" (Matthew 18:3). Brigham Young University president Dallin H. Oaks, later called as one of the Lord's latter-day special witnesses said, "A child loses a treasured possession, prays for help, and is inspired to find it. . . . The Holy Ghost acts in his office . . . communicating information and truths for the edification and guidance of the recipient" (*Brigham Young University 1981–82 Devotional and Fireside Speeches* [Provo, Utah: University Press, 1982], 20–26).

Perhaps a cynic would say that finding "Boyd's car" was just a matter of chance, but it would be hard to convince

Boyd of that. In fact, from that time on, Boyd didn't refer to the car as being his; instead, he called it "Jesus' car." This little blue station wagon served as a reminder that God loved him and that his prayer had been heard. Through his faith, that which had been lost had been returned. Through this simple experience, his relationship with his Heavenly Father had been strengthened. Notice how viewing himself as connected to his Heavenly Father changed the way he interpreted the physical world around him, even the way he viewed his toys.

I wonder if we who have made sacred covenants in sacred places fully understand the power of rising above our personal ownership agenda to recognize that all that we have—all of our toys, houses, cars, boats, money, and even our bodies—belong to that God who gave us life. If we capture this vision, then our own interpretation of the physical world around us is more likely to take on the concept of consecration.

As Elder Jeffrey R. Holland has said, "We cannot then say in ignorance or defiance, 'Well, it's my life' or worse yet, 'It's my body.' It is not. 'Ye are not your own,' Paul said [1 Corinthians 6:13–20]. 'Ye are bought with a price'" (Jeffrey R. Holland and Patricia T. Holland, *On Earth As It Is in Heaven* [Salt Lake City: Deseret Book, 1994], 188).

It was not enough for Boyd to understand that his car was in the hands of his Savior. That car was just an object lesson, teaching him that his body and the events that were shortly to come in that body were in the Savior's hands as well.

Another of the Lord's special witnesses has taught that to *know* is not to follow, but to *know* and to *love* is to follow (Neal A. Maxwell, "'According to the Desire of [Our] Hearts,'" *Ensign,* November 1996, 21–23). I had hopes that when it came time for Boyd to walk through the veil of this life into the next life that his love for his Heavenly Father and his Savior would allow him to do so without fear of the babysitter.

The events that took place through the rest of Boyd's life provided a kind of "Jesus' car" experience for Arlene and me. We had the still, small reminders that just as our son's car was returned to him following a season of absence, the Lord is ever mindful of each of his children. Even those who may be separated from their families by death can be returned to the bosom of their loved ones once again.

Another experience likewise became one of these still, small reminders. My senior year at Brigham Young University was a financial struggle for my wife and me. The medical bills that we had accumulated were overwhelming, to say the least. This was about six months before Spencer was born. Oddly enough, this experience happened around the same time as Boyd's encounter with "Jesus' car."

It was Christmastime, but we barely had enough money to get by, with none left over for the joys of purchasing presents during the yuletide season. Like so many married students, Arlene and I were getting through each day by focusing on the tomorrows that we hoped for after graduation. Boyd's projected life span was a constant reminder that this kind of thinking didn't always apply. That year we didn't even have enough money for a Christmas tree.

Even though I was driving around Utah County witnessing the Christmas cheer all around me, I was overshadowed with a gloom that I just couldn't seem to escape. I couldn't help thinking that if the medical doctors were right, then Boyd might not experience many more Christmas seasons.

I could live for a better day down the road when we could provide a more traditional Christmas for our children, but I could not bear the fear that Boyd might not be there to celebrate it with us. I wanted him to have at least the joy of a Christmas tree in the front room, even if there were no presents under it.

Many students at Brigham Young University buy Christmas trees and throw them away a few weeks before the actual holiday because they go home to their families between semesters. Because of this, the dumpsters behind student housing are filled with trees about mid-December. I swallowed my pride and crept behind the dorms late one night to pick up a tree for my family out of one of the dumpsters.

You can imagine what the tree looked like after students had purchased it from a lot, placed it in the trunk of their car, removed the tree from their vehicle, and then carefully pulled it through their doorway. Next, they followed the tradition of setting it up on a stand and hanging all of the traditional ornaments and lights. After a few weeks of enjoyment, they removed the ornaments and dragged the tree from their warm apartment, through the doorway, and out to the garbage bin, where they recklessly threw it into the dumpster with no expectation that it would ever be used again. There it sat for a few cold days and icy Utah nights, until I came along and carefully rescued it from its hiding place.

I completed the task and then drove away from the dumpster, hoping that no one had seen me. My motivation for this misadventure came from a heart that seemed to be breaking inside me as I thought of the meager Christmas I was providing for my family. As I drove toward my apartment, I continually demanded of myself, "Is this the best you can do?" Boyd and Preston were so young they wouldn't complain, but it still weighed heavily on my mind as I made my way home. By the time I carefully pulled the tree out of the trunk of the car and through my doorway and placed it in my front room, it looked more like a yuletide skeleton than a Christmas tree.

After pouring white flour all over it in hopes of giving it the look of snow, we proceeded to make paper angels, as well as a few ornaments from dough, to hang on the limbs. We then made popcorn, and using a needle and thread, we created a long string of those fluffed-up kernels, which were then wrapped around the tree from top to bottom. I am not exaggerating when I say that, at best, the tree looked pathetic. When my sons started eating the popcorn and brushing against the tree, they compounded the problem. Most of the white flour fell off the anemic limbs to the floor. It didn't help matters when we swept up the white flour and sprayed the limbs with water from an old Windex bottle, with the expectation that we could then shower the flour on the tree and get it to stick to the moist limbs rather than fall to the floor again. While it is true that more of the flour stayed on the limbs, it was also true that it didn't have the appearance of snow. It looked like what it was—wet flour sitting in clumps on the limbs, which were little more than sticks. Spraying the tree with water did little to improve the paper angels either.

There the tree stood at attention, as straight as it could, as if it were trying to make up for the fact that there were no presents at its base. (A year later we were reminded of our foolish attempt at snow when we brought out the dough ornaments we had made, only to discover that they were filled with weevils from the white flour.)

As I stood gazing at this sad work of art, I tried to elevate my thoughts. "Christmas is a time for giving of yourself and of celebrating the birth of our Savior." I tried to comfort myself with that thought, but I still felt remorse because I could not even afford gifts for our children.

After sharing a few Christmas stories, we tucked our children in bed. I could not sleep, so I walked about the apartment wishing that I could provide just a little more for my family. I did not want to keep up with the Joneses. I just wanted to give our children a little taste of the kind of Christmas that I had experienced as a child, with just a few presents. I wanted Boyd to have at least one Christmas like that. As I offered my evening prayer, I petitioned Heavenly Father that while I accepted where Boyd was in his life, I wished that I could give him just a little more to comfort him and bring him joy. There would be other Christmas seasons for our two-year-old Preston, when we would be settling down as a family following graduation. But what about Boyd? I went to bed that night with those thoughts weighing heavily on my mind.

In the morning we awoke and went about our day. It felt odd not to see children opening presents and screaming with joy at what they had found. Our day began as it always had: giving Boyd a treatment. Afterward, I headed for the front door to empty the trash. As I opened it, my eyes caught hold of something at my feet—a basket of oranges. Thinking of my prayer the night before, a Scroogelike thought flashed through my mind: "He's got the whole world in his hands and he gives me oranges." With a sigh, I reached down.

With a nod to my better nature, I accepted the oranges as a nice gesture from an anonymous neighbor, and I brought the basket in the house. As the day progressed, Boyd and

Preston found great use for this fruit. They attempted every activity that they could think of for one or more oranges. After a few hours, I reached into the basket to replace an orange that had been eaten. As I did so, my eye caught hold of something. Just below the orange I was touching, I beheld two crisp fifty-dollar bills. I could not believe what I was seeing. My mind quickly went back to the night before and the petition I had made to my Heavenly Father, as well as to my sarcastic thought when I had found the basket on the front porch.

As we searched for an open store where we could buy some food and a few presents for the children, I was thankful that the Lord had heard my prayer. I was grateful for the wonderful, anonymous Samaritan who had followed the promptings of the still, small voice in order to give us a reminder that "Jesus' car" experiences can happen to daddies as well as to sons. Just as Boyd was convinced of the Lord's hand in finding his car, I was, and still am, persuaded that God heard my prayer and provided a star for me to follow on that Christmas day many years ago. As simple as the experience was, it reinforced the idea that the Lord is mindful of all aspects of our daily lives.

7

PREPARATION

I'm sure there were times when Boyd's body seemed to be a prison for him. Most of the time he was as active as his friends, but as he grew older, he didn't have quite the get-up-and-go that youthful living demands. Also, the daily respiratory treatments were restraining at times for him. The trips to the hospital with the shots, blood tests, IV needles, and constant medical care didn't make life in his body any easier. Even though life was good for Boyd most of the time, he lived with the expectation that one day he would receive his resurrected body. This was the logical extension to the concept of the complete self that he had learned early in life.

During the time we lived in American Fork, shortly after Spencer was born, we had an incident that proved to be an excellent teaching moment. We acquired a parakeet that we named Penelope. Boyd, nearly four years old, and Preston, two years old, took great delight in the antics of their little pet. Their most enjoyable times occurred on warm days, when we would place Penelope's cage on the back porch. But even in the summer, Utah evenings can get a little chilly for a parakeet, so we brought her into the kitchen each night.

One particular evening, I forgot to bring the cage inside. In the morning, Arlene quickly corrected my mistake, but our pet never fully recovered. After Penelope fell down a few times, we placed a lamp nearby her cage. The warmth seemed to revive her for a time and she flew back onto her perch. However, this success was short-lived, and soon she died.

I chose this moment to review the doctrine of resurrection with Boyd. All parents must deal with a situation like this in a sensitive manner according to the needs of their children. It is easy in the hustle and bustle of all the things that must be done in the adult world to miss simple teaching moments like this one. It is also easy to delegate this responsibility to the Primary or Sunday School teacher. However, the consequences of assuming that our children will know and understand the doctrines of the kingdom at someone else's feet is risky parenting at best. Even though I am a teacher myself, I fully understand that the responsibility lies with the parent. To be a parent is to be a teacher—that responsibility cannot be delegated.

Boyd and I dug a little hole in the garden and buried Penelope. My words went something like this: "Everyone's body will die. Their spirit goes back to Heavenly Father, who in time returns to them their body in its resurrected or perfected state. After the resurrection the body will never die."

As usual, Boyd listened carefully, but it was so difficult to know just where he was in terms of likening the concept of resurrection to himself. From time to time, as Boyd noticed his own body giving way to cystic fibrosis, he would make comments like, "Someday my body will be resurrected, and I won't have to have treatments anymore." I hoped that he wasn't just repeating our words. My desire was that the Lord, through the Spirit, was also instructing and preparing him beyond our limited abilities for that which was to come. For most of us this realization is a natural evolution of aging, but Boyd's illness brought the need for resurrection to his mind much sooner than it would have normally evolved.

In December 1979, I completed my schooling at Brigham Young University. Our joy increased when I was accepted as a seminary teacher for The Church of Jesus Christ of Latter-day Saints. Arlene and I experienced a great deal of anxiety when we traveled to the Church Office Building in Salt Lake City to find out where we would be sent. When we were told our assignment was Phoenix, Arizona, we looked at each other with an expression that said, "Where's that?" Beyond recognizing the name and where it was on the map, neither of us had ever had much experience with the Southwest. The only thing I knew about Phoenix was that it was where the Phoenix Suns basketball team played its home games. The only thing Arlene had heard about Phoenix was that it was hot.

With this background, we took our family and all our dreams to Arizona. The great people of Phoenix and the surrounding areas helped create a wonderful home for us. Except for the effect of the penetrating heat on Boyd in the spring and summer, living in this area was all we could have hoped for.

We were open in our conversations with Boyd concerning his body. Without being morbid or too commonplace, we spoke periodically about death. We referred to it not as the end of life but as the beginning of a new era in our lives. We talked of living with Heavenly Father and our departed loved ones and of what it might be like in our resurrected body. We had numerous conversations about what everyday life might be like in heaven, always trying to stay within the revealed truth of the gospel, rather than indulge in idle fantasies or our own opinions.

Although we were enjoying every moment in mortality with our son and were trying to help him find fulfillment in each day, we also felt the need to place his short life in an eternal perspective. By truly understanding this, he would not feel handicapped or cheated by life in his body. The words of Elder Dallin H. Oaks capture much of what we wanted our son to understand: "The assurance of resurrection and immortality affects how we look on the physical challenges of mortality, how we live our mortal lives, and how we relate to those around us. The assurance of resurrection gives us the strength and perspective to endure the mortal challenges faced by each of us . . . , such things as the physical, mental, or emotional deficiencies we bring with us at birth or acquire during mortal life. Because of the resurrection, we know that these mortal deficiencies are only temporary!" ("Resurrection," *Ensign,* May 2000, 15).

It is hard for many of us to grasp this concept while our bodies are in their prime. For the aged and the handicapped, however, this doctrine gives understanding, perspective, and patience in the difficult season of life they may be passing through in a body that is not as active as they would wish. Barring a quick exit from life as the result of an accident, even those with the most active bodies will have to face that season eventually. For those who feel that they are in the final chapter of their lives, there is a yearning to understand what lies beyond the door of mortality. Such was the case for Boyd.

One day Arlene, Boyd, and I spent a warm Phoenix afternoon visiting our stake president and friend, Widtsoe Shumway, who owned a mortuary on the west side of Phoenix. After leaving his office, we decided to walk through the burial grounds. We looked at the grave markers and tried to guess the style of clothes and the way of life these people had during the time they lived on earth. As we walked along, Boyd asked, "Dad, who do you think will go to live with Heavenly Father first, me or you?"

I replied, "I don't know for sure, Boyd. What do you think?"

"I think I will." He then turned to his mom and asked, "When am I going to live with Heavenly Father?"

She said, "Are you getting anxious, Boyd?"

After pondering her question, he said, "Yes."

Though Boyd was fully aware of his physical situation, his answer surprised us. Even at the tender age of six, he was able to discern that his death was near. It has been my experience that it is not unusual for an individual who is near death, no matter what his age, to find the veil is thin in this regard. I suppose that would not be surprising to anyone whose body is going through those stages that prepare us to pass on to the other side.

Boyd's response was not unlike an experience repeated many times by President David O. McKay concerning former United States president John Quincy Adams. While in the twilight of his life, Adams met an acquaintance as he strolled down a street in Boston.

A friend accosted him and said: "Mr. Adams, how are you?" Confident that he would live after his body had ceased to function in the physical world, the venerable man replied: "Thank you, sir! John Quincy Adams himself is well, sir, quite well. I thank you. But the house I live in at present is becoming dilapidated. It is tottering on its foundation. Time and seasons have nearly destroyed it. Its roof is pretty well worn out. Its walls are much shattered, and it trembles with every wind. The old tenement is becoming almost uninhabitable, and I think John Quincy Adams will have to move out soon: but he, himself, is quite well, sir, quite well." (David O. McKay, *Gospel Ideals: Selections from the Discourses of David O. McKay,* ed. G. Homer Durham [Salt Lake City: Improvement Era, 1953], 57)

John Quincy Adams's self-image obviously went beyond the physical reflection he saw in the mirror. His view of self had a perspective that went much deeper than his own body. He understood that age, fashion, and the opinions of others eventually create a losing battle for the person whose self-concept is entirely physical. As important as the mortal body is, it is a preparatory stage to school us for the crowning acquisition of our resurrected tabernacle. At this point we could only hope that Boyd was emotionally and spiritually ready. It was becoming obvious as each day passed that he was more and more prepared physically for this transition.

It was not enough to prepare Boyd to meet his Maker; we also faced a challenge in preparing our four-year-old son, Preston, for the loss of his older brother. Preston had an experience that made us wonder if he would be able to handle Boyd's passing.

Our next-door neighbor's house became the center of excitement when they added a litter of kittens to their family.

Because our dog, Buffy, delighted in chasing cats, we were a bit concerned for their safety. We told Preston he was free to visit the kittens all he wanted but to make sure not to bring any of them home.

A few days after we laid down the law, Preston cupped his hands around one of the cuddly little kittens and brought it home. Preston loved Buffy and he loved the kittens, so it was only natural for him to want them to meet. With the joy of a loving child sharing the wonder of life, he searched the yard for his dog. At the sound of his voice, Buffy came running. As Preston held out his new friend, Buffy leaped forward and knocked the kitten from his grasp. Buffy instantly destroyed the kitty as Preston watched in horror.

A friend of ours, who was babysitting, heard the commotion and ran to Preston's aid. He found our stunned child, his eyes glazed in shock, clutching the dead kitten. Preston turned to the babysitter and announced in a subdued tone, "The kitty is just asleep."

Our guest gently removed the kitten from his grasp. As he buried it in the backyard, Arlene arrived to comfort our little son. He continued to state, "It's just sleeping, it's just sleeping."

This reaction was understandable—not just in the sense that he couldn't face the death of the kitty, but he might also have had some fears that he would be punished for bringing it home. As the days passed, we became concerned that he still couldn't accept the fact that the kitten was dead. We worried because of Boyd's fragile health and feared that his death might affect Preston in the same way.

A few weeks later, Preston had an experience that eased some of our fears concerning his ability to accept Boyd's imminent passing. Like so many other children, Preston had a fascination for bugs and small animals, which he found in the garden or the lawn. He would capture a little critter and run for an authority figure to identify his find.

After a morning of playing in the yard, he brought in a little bird that had fallen out of a nest located in a tree in front of the house. Arlene was concentrating on one of her many household duties and didn't notice Preston enter the room. He thrust his hands up in the direction of her face and said, "Mama, look!"

Arlene turned and found herself gazing eyeball to eyeball with a little chirping bird that was just about as startled as she was. After catching her breath, she examined Preston's new-found friend. The poor bird was so new to this world that it had not yet grown feathers.

Preston and Boyd decided they would become the adopted parents of their tiny friend. The new home for the bird was an Easter basket lined with paper towels. With Arlene's help, they fed the bird milk and wheat grass juice through an eye-dropper. Although she didn't tell them at the time, Arlene felt sure that the little bird wouldn't recover. This featherless creature was so weak and pale that as it received each feeding, we could actually see the liquid filling its stomach. Still, the boys were determined to help their friend get well.

Arlene wisely decided not to string their hopes on too long. After a day she told them the bird was just too sick and was going to die. In an effort to comfort his little friend, Boyd leaned over it and said, "Don't be afraid, little bird. When you die you'll get a new body and won't be sick any more."

Preston just couldn't quite accept this. He looked at Boyd and then turned back to the bird with different words of comfort: "Pretty soon you'll grow feathers and fly away."

To our surprise, the bird hung on for a day or two. Boyd's own breathing at this time was so labored that he required the assistance of a small, portable oxygen tank. A thin tube stretched from the tank and connected to his nose.

After breakfast one morning, Boyd watched the bird intently, while Arlene stood at the sink doing the dishes. Suddenly, he said, "Mom, this bird looks just like me."

She stopped and watched the bird with Boyd. Its chest was heaving up and down much more than she had noticed before. Instantly, she made the connection between the bird and Boyd. She quickly turned away from Boyd, shielding him from her emotions. With a lump in her throat, she returned to the sink.

Boyd repeated his observation. "Mom, this bird does look just like me."

Arlene knew all too well that Boyd was in much the same predicament as this little struggling bird. Fighting back the tears, all she could say was, "I know, Boyd, I know."

The bird was dead before noon. At first, Preston wasn't able to accept this any better than the passing of the kitten. He sat on the couch with the same stunned look on his face we had seen following the incident with our dog Buffy.

Boyd attempted to comfort his little brother by saying, "The bird is not really dead; he just went back to Heavenly Father. He's going to get his brand-new body, and this one will have feathers!"

He must have said the right thing because in a short time Preston perked up. Our oldest son's timely counsel was a great support for Preston in preparing him for the events that were to come in the next few days.

Of course, a person's attitude and mind-set rarely change as quickly as in the story I have just told. I'm sure this was true even for Preston—and all of us in the family, for that matter. As hard as we work, and as much as we may prepare ourselves to lose someone close to us, a certain amount of trial, error, pain, tears, and grief is unavoidably associated with the loss of a loved one. There is no way we can prepare ourselves for this event in such a fashion that there will be no pain following the death of those we love. The deep feelings and struggles associated with death are normal and should be expected. Not experiencing these emotions would require some form of avoidance behavior or denial (see Appendix, 181).

8

The Fingerprint of the Lord

lthough Boyd had been using oxygen for nearly three months, he was able to remove the tube from his nose for short periods of time if he wanted to be a little more mobile. The evening after the bird passed away, Arlene had an experience that helped us understand how close Boyd was to the end of his mortal sojourn.

As she was bathing him in the tub, he became silent and just stared straight ahead with a glazed look in his eyes. After a brief inspection, she realized the oxygen tank was empty. As she reached for the doorknob in preparation for replacing the tank, she relaxed her grip on Boyd for just an instant. Immediately, he fell forward, smacking his head on the side of the tub. While holding Boyd, she yelled for help. A friend who was visiting at the time came running to her assistance. With this added help, she quickly changed oxygen tanks.

Connecting a new tank was like plugging in a toy doll.

Boyd sat up and carried on as if nothing had happened. By this time, his forehead had a huge purple lump on it. As Arlene removed him from the tub, she said, "I'm sorry, Boyd, about the bump on your head."

He replied, "What bump, Mom?"

She held him up to the mirror so he could see the bump. To her surprise, he was unable to remember the incident at all. This sudden, total dependency on oxygen shocked us, and it became obvious how quickly his health was failing. Arlene held Boyd in the rocking chair long after he had fallen asleep, treasuring each remaining moment with her son.

Each morning, when I arose to get ready for work, Boyd tried his best to get up and visit with me before I left. This little ritual was a boost to my spirits and a bonding time for my son and me. The day following Boyd's bump on the head, true to form, he got out of bed and sat on the floor of the bathroom while I shaved.

That particular morning, he asked a question that made me realize how tough life had become for him: "Dad, can you breathe?"

After pausing a moment, I cast a discerning look down at him. "Yes, I can, son. Why do you ask?"

The look in his eyes broke my heart as he said simply, "It's hard for me."

I had no counsel to offer at this point. I knelt down and held my son, wondering how many mornings we would have left together. By the evening his condition had worsened.

After the children were tucked in bed, Arlene sat on Boyd's bed as he struggled to sleep. His breathing was so difficult that the only way he could be comfortable was to lie face down with his knees tucked up to his chest. He used his knees and his arms as a kind of shock absorber to keep the pressure of the bed off his chest. This little maneuver helped to maximize his ability to breathe.

He would sleep for a while and then wake up with a jolt in the middle of a coughing spell. This happened repeatedly for a few hours until, in desperation, he turned to Arlene and said, "Mom, what can I do so I won't keep waking up, waking up, waking up?"

She replied, "Boyd, I don't know what I can do for you."

He continued, "Then where can I sleep where I won't keep waking up, waking up, waking up?"

Arlene mourned aloud, "Oh, Boyd, I wish I knew!"

She came into our room as I was preparing to go to bed and related Boyd's words to me. After pondering a moment, we realized that we were helpless. This feeling of being in totally unfamiliar territory drove us to our knees.

We knelt together and prayed with all the faith we could gather that our son wouldn't have to suffer unnecessarily. We petitioned Heavenly Father that if this was Boyd's time, to please take him home. I'm sure that a portion of our petition had to do with our own feelings of inadequacy. We were not sure about our own ability to endure our son's suffering.

I hope that our pleading was in the same spirit spoken of by Elder Neal A. Maxwell: "Heavenly Father not only expects but also encourages us to plead with Him over our challenges. Our pleading is not a sign of weakness, but can reflect thoughtful submissiveness. Indeed, Jesus, who knew clearly what He faced in Gethsemane and on Calvary, nevertheless pleaded with the Lord for the cup to be removed from Him. Therefore it is what we do during and after the pleading that matters, especially as to our submissiveness to the Lord. But pleadings are appropriate" (Neal A. Maxwell, *One More Strain of Praise* [Salt Lake City: Bookcraft, 1999], 8).

I went to bed while Arlene tended to Boyd. We always tried to be positive and cheerful in front of Boyd, but as Arlene lay next to him watching him suffer, she couldn't stop the tears from flowing. Typical of Boyd, he reached over and patted her on the back—mother and son in this most difficult moment, trying their best to comfort each other.

During the night, at Arlene's request, I gave Boyd a priesthood blessing. This blessing was like so many others I had given him. I blessed him that he would rest comfortably through the night. Numerous nights of discomfort for Boyd evolved into restful sleep with the aid of the priesthood. This power has been a great support in our home.

We decided that if Boyd's condition didn't improve, we would take him to the hospital the next day. Arlene stayed with Boyd through the night. He rested easier but still struggled considerably with his breathing. She knelt next to him and prayed without ceasing. She pleaded that if Boyd's life was coming to a close, the Lord would take him quickly without suffering. After petitioning the Lord in this manner for many hours, she fell asleep.

At times like these it is easy to ask, "Why me? Why my son? What have we done to deserve such a fate?" What a blessing it is to have the gospel of Jesus Christ to give us the strength to endure and the peace to carry on (see Appendix, 183). We had taught Boyd about the eternal nature of life—this was a time for us to hold fast to those teachings ourselves.

Sometime during the night, while lying next to Boyd in

the most difficult of circumstances, Arlene had a dream in which she saw Boyd at the hospital in the care of two physicians she had never met before. The dream seemed insignificant at the time, but it was accompanied by a peaceful feeling.

The reason she felt the dream had no real meaning was that in each of Boyd's hospital visits over the past two years, the cystic fibrosis patients had been solely in the hands of one fine doctor, who cared a great deal for Boyd and the other children. In Arlene's mind, she could see no purpose in replacing our doctor, but she could not ignore the comforting spirit that came with the dream.

As the morning arrived, Boyd's condition had not improved. He was dizzy and struggled for breath continually. This time he was the one who suggested a visit to the hospital. He seemed to know when the medication and treatments we gave him at home were not enough. Staying in the hospital was trying for Boyd, but he had the maturity to recognize when a stay was needed. So while I went to work at the seminary, Arlene took him to the hospital.

To her surprise, as she entered the pediatric ward, she was greeted by the same two physicians she had seen the night before in her dream. Arlene felt the same calming spirit that she had during her dream. As she moved through the preliminary introductions and procedures, her thoughts continued to review meeting these two men in her dream the night before. Although she was a stranger to them, she knew them.

Later in the day I joined Arlene at the hospital. A number of tests had been completed and the doctors wanted to talk with us before proceeding any further. Arlene waited patiently in the consulting room for me to arrive.

As I entered the room, I was surprised not to be greeted by our normal physician. She had been called away for the weekend to a conference in San Francisco. As we visited with these men, I was amazed to discover that they were both active brethren of our own faith.

I recognized this as a rare occurrence outside Utah. Arlene recognized it as a fulfillment of the dream she had experienced the night before. Now she understood why the Lord had replaced our doctor with these two men. We had prayed the night before that the Lord would allow this difficult moment in our son's life to pass quickly. To strengthen us at this most difficult time, the Lord surrounded us with these two priesthood brethren. As the years have passed, my wife and I have reflected on that event. We have always been grateful, at that terribly trying time, that the Lord would place us in the hands of doctors who had the priesthood as well as an eternal perspective. We had prayed for strength, and the Lord gave us just that, in the form of these two angels.

A few years later, I happened to see one of these doctors while attending church in Mesa, Arizona. He rehearsed with me the unusual nature of what had happened. He told me that a medical convention was being held in San Francisco and, at the last minute, the director of the hospital in Phoenix insisted that our regular physician should hand over her duties for a few days and attend the convention. This LDS doctor believed that the inspiration that sent our doctor to California may have had less to do with the convention than it did with Boyd's circumstances. In times like these, if we can see clearly, it may not be so difficult to witness the fingerprint of the Lord in our lives.

After a short visit, they told us that, in their opinion, Boyd had a very short time before he would pass away. They felt his life would not extend much longer than a week. However, they were committed to work with Boyd through the night, and the following morning they would repeat the tests to see if he had improved. If there was no change for the better, they would counsel with us again. As Boyd's parents, we would have the opportunity to make a difficult decision—whether to continue the medical treatments in the hope of sustaining his life as long as possible or cease the treatment and thereby end his struggle without extending his suffering any further. We felt the support of these kind men as they left us alone to discuss their advice.

It was at this time that I began to recognize the Lord's comforting spirit in regard to Boyd's passing. When Boyd was born, it was easy to feel a divine force present during the birth itself. I have also felt this in witnessing the birth of our other children. I felt that someone much greater than either my wife or me was monitoring and influencing the birth of our children. With an even greater impact, I sensed the Lord's influence during Boyd's passing. In an odd sort of way, I felt that others who were waiting on the other side of the veil to welcome our son home could think of what we called death as a kind of birth. President Wilford Woodruff identified this same idea many years ago: "I cannot help but think that in every death there is a birth; the spirit leaves the body. . . . And passes to the other side of the veil alive" *(Discourses of Wilford Woodruff, Fourth President of The Church of Jesus Christ of Latter-day Saints,* ed. G. Homer Durham [Salt Lake City: Bookcraft, 1946], 245). President David O. McKay placed death in its eternal perspective when he said, "To the Savior of the world there is no such thing as death—only life—

eternal life" (David O. McKay, *Gospel Ideals: Selections from the Discourses of David O. McKay,* ed. G. Homer Durham [Salt Lake City: Improvement Era, 1953], 58).

Following the counsel of the doctors, Arlene and I knelt together once again and prayed in behalf of our son. We asked Heavenly Father, "If this is Boyd's time to go, please let him be alert long enough to have a comforting visit with the whole family."

As I look back now, this desire seems somewhat out of place or even a bit selfish. Our rationale behind the prayer was that we wanted Preston's and Spencer's last living memory of their brother to be a happy experience. The past few weeks had been taxing on the family, and Boyd had been so sick that he was just not able to interact with his brothers the way he normally had done. The past few hours he was almost comatose and difficult even to arouse. Preston and Spencer had been somewhat lost in the shuffle of events, and we were hoping they might have the opportunity to have some kind of closure in their relationship with their older brother.

Immediately after praying we went to Boyd's room. He was sitting up in bed visiting quite comfortably with Preston, Spencer, and an adult friend of ours. Boyd hadn't been this alert for several days. We laughed and visited with him for about twenty minutes, which was like a miracle to us. What a contrast to the way he had been the past few weeks. It was as if he had been brought back from the brink of death for one last visit with the family. This last family home evening with our boys might only be equaled by the next one we have on the other side of the veil. What a wonderful blessing from the Lord to give our family this last moment together.

At the conclusion of our visit, Arlene took the rest of

the family home. I was going to spend the night with Boyd. Immediately after they left, Boyd took a deep breath—almost a sigh. He then lay back down and resumed the same disposition he had maintained when we brought him in. It was almost as if when had Arlene left the room, she reached back inside the doorway to turn off the light switch, and at that same moment a light was also turned off inside Boyd. Except for a few precious moments, he never regained the level of awareness he had shown during this visit with the family.

Through the night there were interruptions for shots, blood tests, and respiratory treatments, but in between Boyd slept with more comfort than he had in weeks. I have no doubt that his visit with the family and his restful sleep were an answer to our prayer. The immediacy with which this prayer was answered was a reminder to me of the immediacy with which God hears all of his children's prayers. Sometimes, when the answers don't come within the time frame we would wish, it is easy to lose sight of the fact that our prayers have been heard and understood. The challenge often is in being able to have faith in the Lord's timing regarding his answer. Indeed, "we cannot have true faith in the Lord without also having complete trust . . . in the Lord's timing" (Dallin H. Oaks, "Faith in the Lord Jesus Christ," *Ensign,* May 1994, 100; see also Appendix, 184).

In the morning, I met with the doctors as planned. The night's work with Boyd had not improved his condition at all. True to their words from the previous night, they asked my advice concerning the plan of action they should take. After a short visit with Arlene on the phone, I returned to the doctors.

Perhaps only a parent can feel the full weight of this

moment. I'm not sure I can adequately communicate my feelings as I gave my permission to let Boyd go. As painful as this was for us, we felt it was best for Boyd. I could not have given my permission without the total support of my sweet wife. In fact, I'm sure I could not have suggested anything to the doctors unless Arlene and I were completely agreed in our feelings regarding the matter.

Oh, the importance of a testimony in my life! Years before, as a new missionary in England, I fasted and prayed to gain a knowledge of the truthfulness of the restored gospel of Jesus Christ. That witness came in such a manner that I could not doubt that it was from my Heavenly Father. Even the passing of time could not erase the witness I had gained as a young man so many years earlier. Without an understanding of the atoning sacrifice of Christ and its effect on Boyd, how could I cast a vote in allowing Boyd to leave mortality at this time? Even with the assurance of the Atonement, I suffered grief and anguish of soul.

The plan was that they would stop all his treatments and drug therapy while giving Boyd something to help him sleep. This would allow him to leave this world with as little discomfort as possible. In making this decision, I felt as shaky as a child taking his first step. Indeed, I was walking in what was, for me, unknown territory, "not knowing beforehand the things which I should do" (1 Nephi 4:6).

After meeting with the doctors, I returned to Boyd's room. I felt that I needed one more chance to visit with my son. I wanted him to understand what was about to happen to him, and I wanted to prepare him for the next step in his eternal progression. Brigham Young said: "We see our youth, even, frequently stubbing their toes and falling down. But yonder [in the spirit world], how different! They move with ease and like lightning. . . . [In mortality], we are continually troubled with ills and ailments. . . . In the spirit world we are free from all this . . . , we shall enjoy the society of the just and the pure who are in the spirit world until the resurrection" (*Discourses of Brigham Young,* sel. John A. Widtsoe [Salt Lake City: Deseret Book, 1954], 380–81). In my own way, I wanted to communicate this to my son.

I decided to continue the conversation I had with him as an infant when I held him up to the mirror to explain the nature of his physical self. Instead of using a mirror, I propped up the head of his bed and peeled back the covers.

My words to him went something like this: "Boyd, take a good look at your body. It's not working very well, is it, son?"

He agreed that it was a source of pain for him at this stage in his life.

I continued, "Are you ready to go home to your Heavenly Father and take the next step in obtaining a resurrected body?"

Boyd smiled faintly and agreed that this would be the wish of his heart.

"I want you to lie back and try to sleep. The doctors are going to come in and give you a shot to help you sleep. You will not have any more treatments or IV therapy or pain of any kind. When you wake up you may be in this room, but you will not be in your body." Because of the conversations we had had throughout his life, he understood that the "you" I was referring to included his spiritual self.

I wanted my son not to be afraid of being alone immediately following his death, so I said, "Boyd, when you wake up, someone will come to be with you [Alma 40:11–12; Ecclesiastes 12:7]. Don't be afraid. You will be filled with peace and love, and you will never again have to experience the kind of pain you are feeling now. In time, you will receive your resurrected body. The rest of the family will join you when our time comes to leave this life."

I did not want him to feel that, in death, he would pass from us to a strange place where he would be alone. I reviewed the concept that the spirit world is right here round about us. If our spiritual eyes were open, we would see others visiting with us and directing us. With all of my heart, I hoped that those who were "directing" Boyd from the other side of the veil would be there for him, welcoming him home like a spiritual family reunion. I hoped that their embrace would overcome the fear that might come to our son upon finding himself in a new environment.

I wanted to communicate to my son that this was not an event to be afraid of. Brigham Young said, "There is no period known to them [the dead] in which they experience so much joy as when they pass through the portals of death, and enter upon the glorious change of the spirit world" (Paul H. Dunn and Richard Eyre, *The Birth That We Call Death* [Salt Lake City: Bookcraft, 1976], 53). It was in this manner that I tried to comfort my son.

A short time later, the doctors came in and gave Boyd a shot to help him sleep. After expressing love to him, I tucked the covers around him, and I said what proved to be my last good-bye to my dear son here in mortality.

As he tried to sleep, my eyes were fixed upon his face. Even though he was "nigh unto death," his expression was not one of sadness. I desperately wanted to understand the expression on his face. His eyes were closed, but he seemed to be focusing on something. It was not a vague expression; it appeared to be a genuine expression of joy regarding something I was struggling to discern. The only thing I can liken it to is that his countenance seemed to be that of a child trying to sleep the night before Christmas in great expectation of an upcoming gift—a new body!

I recall the feelings of my youth the night before special events such as birthdays or Christmas, when I found it difficult to sleep because of the anticipation regarding the presents to be received the next day. In that setting, sleeping with a smile on my face was not only natural but also expected.

Obviously, the thought of Boyd's passing was difficult, but, oh, the comfort the gospel concept of death was to all of us, especially Boyd, at that moment! How fortunate I am that the last time I tucked my son into bed was, for him, like Christmas Eve. That is a present only the Spirit of the Lord could provide.

The feelings of that moment may be best likened to the words of Brigham Young nearly 150 years ago: "How do you feel, . . . when you are filled with the power and love of God? You are just as happy as your bodies can bear. . . . What did the Holy martyrs die for? Because of the promise of receiving bodies, glorified bodies, in the morning of the resurrection. For this they lived, and patiently suffered, and for this they died" (in *Journal of Discourses,* 26 vols. [London: Latter-day Saints' Book Depot, 1854–86], 3:95).

Boyd was obviously not a martyr, but in the setting he was in at this time, he was "just as happy as [his] body [could] bear." Because of the promise of the resurrection, he waited and "patiently suffered." Perhaps only someone in a similar setting can appreciate the effect that the Spirit of the Lord can have on what would have been the darkest moment in parenting.

I was exhausted from the experience of sitting up with Boyd all night, but I couldn't afford to fall asleep. I had to find some way to stay awake. I called Arlene and asked her to be with Boyd while I went home to shower and freshen up a bit.

The following is Arlene's own account (taken from her journal), describing her visit with Boyd while I went home:

> I prayed all the way to the hospital that I might be with Boyd one more time. I had such mixed feelings. My heart was heavy thinking that Boyd would not be with us, yet I thrilled for Boyd that a more peaceful life was awaiting him.
>
> When I arrived at the hospital, Boyd was laboring much more in his breathing, but resting well. Doug had given his okay for the doctors to give Boyd a shot to help him sleep. I was glad he had made the decision because I don't know if I would have been able to make that decision by myself. I so wanted to talk to Boyd again! It had only been one night, but I already missed hearing his voice. Doug looked so tired, so I stayed with Boyd while he went home and showered.
>
> I sat by Boyd's bed and held his hand. His blanket was next to him but not clutched in his hand like I was used to seeing when he slept. I watched his breathing while my mind wandered. I saw myself pregnant with Boyd, and felt the excitement that Doug and I had. I saw myself in the cold labor room, and I recalled the delivery. The unquenchable joy of having a son. The early morning feedings and the struggles with keeping his food down. His being diagnosed with CF at two months, with our tremendous feelings of remorse. I had given him life and

now I could provide milk and love for him to continue his life.

I saw his sweet countenance that won the hearts of everyone when he was very small. I saw his happy baby-hood—crawling and scrambling when he was excited. I saw his sensitivity to others. Even as a child he showed great interest when his playmates were hurt or crying. Then Preston came and a companionship started. I saw him riding his little blue bike with the training wheels. He took such great pride in peddling with one foot. I saw the special times when we read stories. I recalled the times he asked if he could go play with his friend, Jenni, next door. How many times had he asked to go knock on her door? I wouldn't hear that again—I wouldn't hear his cute little voice again.

I saw him sewing little pillows and the many times he interrupted me to thread a needle or tie a knot. I never got impatient when he interrupted me to thread a needle because I was so touched at the joy and pride he received from his activity.

My thoughts were broken as Boyd suddenly gasped for air. He continued to gasp deeply, as if he were scratching for air. His chest was heaving more as I silently watched with emotion swelling inside me. This was more than I could bear. Tears came quickly, and I put my forehead in my hands and sobbed.

I felt my mother's spirit close to me like I have felt in so many important events in my life. [Arlene's mother passed away when Arlene was nine years old.]

I spoke to her, "Mother, I didn't have the privilege of you raising me completely, but I have felt you helping me many times. Please, please come take care of my boy!"

Instantly, I felt completely calm and assured. The emotions of despair, crying out, and then calm had come so quickly that I knew there was more than just human involvement. I felt there were other spirits close. My

mother, Grandma, Doug's father, and perhaps others were
giving support to Boyd and myself." (see Appendix, 185)

9

PANDORA'S BOX

fter showering, I hurried back to the hospital to join
Arlene at Boyd's bedside. We continued to watch our
son and wait. I'm sure most people have sat watching a child they love sleep. Each peaceful breath serves as a
reminder of how much we love them.

However, this occasion was much different for Arlene
and me. As Boyd continued to sleep, we filled our time with
silent meditation, pondering what lay ahead for our son. At
a moment like this, the atoning sacrifice and resurrection of
Jesus, with all the promises that accompany it, are as important as a gasp of air to a drowning man. As a man desperately
fights through the water toward the surface, all other needs
are replaced with just one thought: *Air!* At this moment in
Boyd's life, our Savior was more than a hope—he was the
very air we were breathing. Our quiet meditation continued
for a few more hours.

The rhythmic pattern of Boyd's breathing was interrupted by his attempt at a single breath so different that it drew our attention. It was a deep breath—almost a gasp—followed by a little shiver. The next breath just didn't come.

Immediately, I experienced an emotion that was totally unexpected. It was as if I was a spectator witnessing the conclusion of a difficult marathon that my son had been running for the past six years. Totally exhausted, he had just crossed the finish line. The end of this race was not marked by the cheering of crowds or the receiving of medals but by the removal of his spirit from his body. This unexpected exhilaration lasted only an instant and was quickly replaced with feelings of tremendous grief as I realized that I would not be blessed with his company as long as I remained here in mortality. This realization jolted me back to the present with my son's body lying there before me.

I kissed Boyd and told him I loved him. Then, Arlene and I held each other and wept, frozen in the moment. At times like this, couples in the Church understand that the initial attraction that brought them together is not the only thing that keeps them together. Basic attraction to each other must mature into something deeper, even more bonding, which is the welding of people to covenants made in sacred temples. If not for that, it would only be natural to run from an event like this, which brings so much pain. But there we were, welded together to our son because of the covenants we had made, and we were trying with all our might to cling to one another. Perhaps this is what Nephi meant when he taught that in order to move forward along the strait and narrow path, we must "cling" to the rod of iron (1 Nephi 8:24, 30). Certainly that was involved as we stood there clinging to each other as well as to our belief in the Savior. At such times, clinging to the iron rod is the only way to hold onto it because it becomes so slippery from our tears.

Elder Neal A. Maxwell stated, "The strait and narrow path . . . is a path, not a freeway nor an escalator. Indeed, there are times when the only way the strait and narrow path can be followed is on one's knees!" ("A Brother Offended," *Ensign,* May 1982, 38). We could certainly relate to Elder Maxwell's sentiment.

Boyd's nurse entered the room and, without speaking, put her arms around us; the three of us stood at the foot of my son's bed and silently mourned.

Later, one of the doctors told me that when Boyd received his last shot while conscious, he looked up and meekly thanked the nurse just after she had administered it. Afterward, a few of the nurses, along with one of the doctors, escaped into the council room and shed tears because this little boy who was so sick still had the presence of mind to say "thank you" at such a difficult moment in his life.

These people whose business it was to be with the sick, who had seen little children die before, and who knew the dangers of draining their own emotional reserves when the needs of other patients still must be met, could not refrain from being touched beyond the point of holding back their emotions. I'm grateful that the calluses of reality did not shield their human need to love those whom they served. Boyd's life was blessed by good people such as these who saw him as more than just a patient with cystic fibrosis. Certainly, there was a nurse here or a doctor there who did not fit this mold, but, as a whole, the medical professionals saw our son as more than a CF patient—they treated him with the dignity and respect to which all human beings are entitled. For this we were grateful.

After a minute or two, I walked over to the window of Boyd's hospital room. Leaning against the window, I pondered my testimony of the gospel. Looking through the glass, I said to no one in particular, "If I didn't know the gospel was true, I might hate God right now. But knowing what I know, I am happy for my son."

The scriptures teach us that "little children are alive in Christ" (Moroni 8:12, 19, 22; see also Appendix, 189). I was trying as best I could to cling to this doctrine in this most trying of times.

Even with all the joy the gospel brings, there is a reason that this life has been called a "veil of tears." While it is true that "there is no tragedy in death, but only in sin," it is also true that there can be great sorrow in death even when sin is not present (Spencer W. Kimball, *Faith Precedes the Miracle* [Salt Lake City: Bookcraft, 1973], 101).

Brigham Young said, "Mourning for the righteous dead springs from . . . ignorance. . . . Could we . . . see into eternity, . . . we should have no disposition to weep or mourn" (*Discourses of Brigham Young,* sel. John A. Widtsoe [Salt Lake City: Deseret Book, 1954], 370). Even with everything that the gospel provides for comfort, at that moment my view of eternity must have been shielded because I had an overpowering "disposition to weep [and] mourn."

I turned and surveyed the room. I didn't want to forget anything that had happened here. I walked over to Boyd's bed and pulled the covers up to his chin, as I had so many times before. This would be the last time. I placed the back of my fingers gently against Boyd's cheek and was awakened to the reality that his body had already started to grow cold. This was neither the texture nor temperature I had known. I was reminded of the analogy of the glove I had shared with him concerning his earthly body. Now his spirit had departed and he was gone; what lay before me on the bed was "the glove."

This lifeless little mortal vehicle, which had been the transportation for his spirit here in mortality for six years, had just run out of fuel. My son had moved on to the next phase of his eternal life. He would receive his body again, refueled in its celestial state. I had to console myself for a season with the words of Joseph Smith: "I have . . . children . . . who have gone to a world of spirits. . . . They are only absent for a moment. They are in the spirit, and we shall soon meet again" (*Teachings of the Prophet Joseph Smith,* sel. Joseph Fielding Smith [Salt Lake City: Deseret Book, 1976], 359).

President Joseph F. Smith spoke of the association parents will have during the Millennium following the resurrection of their little ones: "When the mother is deprived of the pleasure and joy of rearing her babe to manhood or womanhood in this life, through the hand of death, that privilege will be renewed to her hereafter, and she will enjoy it to a fuller fruition than it would be possible for her to do here. . . . [Because] it will be with certain knowledge that the results will be without failure; whereas here, the results are unknown until after we have passed the test" (*Gospel Doctrine* [Salt Lake City: Deseret Book, 1975], 452–54).

It is only natural to mourn the loss of a child, but as I have had time to think of Boyd's passing in light of latter-day revelation, I have found a silver lining in the dark cloud. Life has been likened to a race—indeed, those of us traveling along its roads are all part of the human race. If life is a race, then the people who live long lives may be thought of as participating in a long distance race. Continuing the analogy, those who die in their youth would be thought of as sprinters because of the relative short distance of their race here in mortality.

Do the spectators at a track meet value the long-distance race above that of the sprint? Do the spectators or participants lament the short race because of its lack of quantity in time and distance? Certainly not! We base success or failure of the race not upon its length but on the quality of the effort and performance of the participants.

Another dimension to the race is that everyone at the track meet knows that life goes on after the race, regardless of whether it is short or long. Our son had run his sprint, and we had to console ourselves that he had run the race well and that life continued for him at the conclusion of this one short race. But for Boyd, there were other stadiums to run in, even beyond our eyes, and we had to accept that our own race was not yet complete. Our association with our son in the future will be directly connected with our own efforts in the long-distance race we have yet to complete.

President David O. McKay wrote, "We should not think of life in terms of years, especially if we have in mind a successful life. Some men die young though they live to be four score and ten. Others live long though they die [young]" (*True to the Faith: from the Sermons and Discourses of David O. McKay,* comp. Llewelyn R. McKay [Salt Lake City: Bookcraft, 1967], 142).

Arlene picked up Boyd's blanket, which had been such a comfort to him in his times of rest. As we looked down at the side of his bed, our gaze fell upon the portable oxygen tank that had been his constant companion the past few months. Sitting there so rigidly, it also looked as if the life had gone out of it. We saw the little sign by the door, which the hospital places in all the pediatric rooms. It is a picture of a little train with the occupant's name on it. We had seen it so often, but now we were aware that we would never see it again. We kissed Boyd once more and stood at the foot of his bed, feeling exhausted and a bit lost. This was uncharted territory for us. This time we would be leaving the hospital without our son.

The thought came to me that dying was probably the easiest thing Boyd had to do in his life. Unlike the dramatic picture portrayed on television and in the movies, death was "sweet" for Boyd (D&C 42:46). His death was quite a contrast to other deaths I have witnessed in which sin or a tragic misuse of agency was involved. Although we shed many tears, there was an undertone of joy associated with this event because the Spirit of the Lord was there to buoy us up during this most difficult time.

After making arrangements for his body to be taken care of and signing a few papers, there was nothing more for us to do at the hospital. This era of life was finished, and it was time to go home and gather the rest of our family around us.

When Boyd was too sick to do little more than stay in bed, he liked to listen to music. One of his favorite albums was by a group called Bread. A short time after his passing, I was driving by myself in the car when a song from this album he had loved so much came on the radio. I was instantly brought to the reality of our loss—his smile, his touch, his sweet spirit, as well as his courage in the face of pain.

I pulled over to the side of the road and shed tears until

my emotions were dry. Eventually, I took a deep breath and leaned forward in the driver's seat. Gazing through the windshield, I noticed that the old highway I had been traveling on had many huge trees extending in front of me on both sides of the road—their long, green branches bending toward the center. This long-armed foliage seemed to come together in a kind of heavenly embrace. This naturally made a glorious tunnel, with the sun's rays peeping through just enough to create a kaleidoscope of color. These green limbs seemed to be reaching all around me like some kind of heavenly hug. As I sat there, the heavens began to rain ever so slightly, blending so comfortably with my own tears. There in the midst of all that color, I felt such a contrast of emptiness and beauty together in the same space. How can a person feel peace and emptiness at the same time?

The familiar surroundings of home were a constant reminder of Boyd's absence. The empty bed when it came time to tuck the children in at night, the vacant chair at the dinner table, the unused seat belt in the car, the conversations that hung in the air waiting for his thoughts and feelings to be expressed, his laughter, his cry, and so many other things that tied us to our little boy—all seemed to silently reach out for his presence. Even his toys seemed to cry out for his touch—empty and alone, waiting for their friend to come home.

There is an interesting story in Greek mythology regarding the Creation. As a part of this event, a woman was created to be a companion to man. All of the gods gathered together to give the woman special gifts. Her name was Pandora. While the gods were giving Pandora these wonderful gifts, they were also placing all the opposites of each gift, known as evils, in a great box, which was then locked. She was sent, along with the box, to the earth. All went well until her natural curiosity compelled her to open the box, which brought all the evils into the world. Thus the phrase associated with bringing up a negative subject is known as "opening Pandora's box."

Arlene recorded an interesting insight connecting Pandora's box and Boyd's passing:

> Toward the end of Boyd's life at home he was growing more and more uncomfortable. He didn't sleep well anytime, day or night. As his health worsened, my fears and questions increased. In the daytime I was absorbed with Preston's and Spencer's needs, the housework, and keeping Boyd comfortable. But nighttime was difficult because these haunting questions arose in my mind.
>
> When would he die? How difficult would it be? Would I be there? Would I be strong enough to get through it? Along with so many feelings that were so confusing that they had not been made into questions yet.
>
> It didn't seem like a conscious decision, but I had to put a stop to them. I put them aside for now, knowing that I could deal with them better at a later time. This made me free to hold Boyd when he wanted me to or rub his back late at night. Sometimes he just wanted me to talk to him or just be close by if he needed me.
>
> After Boyd's death I knew that I now had the time to open that box of fears and questions. It reminded me of the mythological story of Pandora's box. When I opened it, to my surprise, it was mostly empty. I already had those questions answered with Boyd's passing.
>
> After recognizing that the box wasn't as full as I had expected, I had two thoughts. One was that I was grateful that I had put those fears and questions aside during the time that I could still be of comfort to Boyd. I had no regrets that I had wasted time for myself that I now

wished that I would have spent on Boyd's needs. The other thought was that I had already accepted the plan that the Lord had for Boyd and had faith that he would answer my new set of questions when the time was right.

Now the questions I had to get an answer for were the ones related to how we would live without Boyd. How to fill the big gap that would only be filled by Boyd's sweetness? How to help Preston and Spencer understand the change in our family and help them remember him?

Before Pandora could replace the lid, all the contents of the box had escaped except one. The last element of the box was *hope.* The gods had included this wonderful gift among all the evils. It was the only one in the box that had failed to escape, so that whatever ills beset Pandora, she could still cling to hope. Arlene and I have realized that there were times in Boyd's life and death that the only thing we had to hold on to was hope. We found it amazing that through those dark seasons it was enough, if only because it was tied to Christ.

Now that Boyd was gone, the time had come for us to open the box as a family and deal with its contents. As difficult as the contents were at the moment, they proved to be a blessing over time, when each was connected to that saving element of the box—hope in Christ.

10

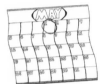

SEIZE THE DAY

ur bishop, Mac Thompson, and his wife, Tyra, were taking care of Preston and Spencer for the day. We pulled into the driveway as Bishop Thompson was preparing to return to the hospital. As we told him of Boyd's passing, we saw a look in his eyes that we would see in the eyes of many of our friends over the next few weeks. There was grief at Boyd's passing and sorrow for us, his family, but also joy for him because he had completed his journey through life. We were overwhelmed by the loving support of our friends in the days following his death.

We were surprised that our friends who seemed to mourn the most were those who had intended to do something for Boyd during the past few weeks but for one reason or another had been unable to follow through.

The day after Boyd's death, a dear lady came to our home with tears streaming down her face. A few weeks before, she had asked what she could do for Boyd. Arlene said he needed some extra activity to keep him from becoming bored and she could come by and read to him. One thing after another had come up, and she was unable to come by. Now the time had passed, and she felt that she had let Boyd down. Arlene put her arms around this wonderful sister as she tried to deal with the anguish of regret.

Another sister from the Church felt that she had let us down because Arlene had called a few times in the last little while and asked if Preston could come over and play with her children. At the time, she had not been able to accommodate Arlene's needs. She felt so bad that she had not adjusted her schedule so that she could have taken a little pressure off Arlene.

Perhaps the incident that got me thinking the most about regret for good deeds left undone involved a wonderful man who had been assigned as a social worker to care for our family over the previous months. I was completely unaware that this assignment had been made. I knew this man and was aware that he had done many wonderful things for a number of people, but I did not know of his assignment in our behalf.

On the day of Boyd's funeral, I was in the back of the house when my brother, Niels (visiting from California), poked his head in the doorway and said, "Doug, your social worker is here to see you."

His words caused my mind to race as I walked toward the front of the house. As I walked by my brother, I responded, "Social worker? I didn't know I had a social worker."

As soon as I had said this, I turned the corner and nearly bumped into my social worker. It was obvious by the look on his face that he had heard my words. A sudden flow of emotion made it difficult for him to speak. Fighting back the tears, he said, "I have been assigned to your family for a number of months now. Can you ever forgive me for not being here when you needed me?"

I had no bitterness in my heart for him. On the contrary, I felt bad that my words had acted like a neon sign announcing his absence. There seemed to be no way to comfort this good man; his mourning for Boyd was compounded by the unique pain that comes from good intentions left dangling. He had procrastinated these past few months, and now he seemed intent on punishing himself for it. His sorrow was the reflection of a good man who was dealing with the regret of letting down people for whom he cared.

I did not feel that he had let us down, but I could see in his eyes a feeling similar to one I have felt on numerous occasions when I have not followed promptings as a religious instructor or have procrastinated my home teaching or have incorrectly ordered my priorities as a husband and father.

A few others came by, also expressing feelings that they had somehow let Boyd or us down. We were taken completely by surprise because we had absolutely no ill feelings toward these friends. We couldn't help but notice how their grief at Boyd's passing was compounded by their feelings of regret, however.

President Spencer W. Kimball had a reminder on his desk in the form of a plaque that read simply, "Do It Now." He expanded on this idea by stating: "One of the most serious human defects in all ages is procrastination, an unwillingness to accept personal responsibilities *now*. . . . There are even many members of the Church who are lax and careless and who continually procrastinate. . . . One Church member of my acquaintance said, . . . 'The Lord knows my heart is right and that I have good intentions. . . . ' But will one receive eternal life on the basis of his good intentions? . . . Samuel Johnson remarked that 'hell is paved with good intentions.' The Lord will not translate one's good hopes and desires and intentions into works. Each of us must do that for himself" (*The Miracle of Forgiveness* [Salt Lake City: Bookcraft, 1969], 8–9).

It was easy for me to see that I too had been guilty so many times of putting my own responsibilities on hold. I have learned in my own life that procrastination oftentimes may be nothing more than the residue of misplaced priorities. The following experience that I had just before Boyd passed away illustrates this point quite well:

Through the years, I have found that participating in activities with my students outside the classroom has enhanced my teaching. It has been my habit to playing basketball with my students a few days each week. This has helped me bring some young people into the classroom by developing a relationship with them on the court. While this may seem a worthwhile venture, on one pivotal occasion it proved to be somewhat misguided.

After school, while I was in the midst of a wonderful basketball game with some of my students, as well as a few nonmembers from school, Arlene called to give me the news that Boyd was not doing well and asked me to give her a ride to the hospital.

At the time, Arlene's request was difficult for a number of reasons, including my selfish perspective that the boys and I were in the middle of an excellent game. However, the deciding factor was the fact that adult supervision was required for the young people to play, and I was the only adult present. So, if I left, the game would then be over, the fun would end, and my more noble excuse of connecting with our nonmember friends would be aborted.

With this logic, I asked my wife to get a ride with a neighbor, and I would meet her at the hospital later. If I had been thinking sensibly, I would have recognized that Arlene was not just asking for a ride—she was requesting my support as well as my companionship. My priority should have been with my wife and son rather than with my students. As it turned out, this was the last time we took Boyd to the hospital, and he was dead within the next few days. Somehow, that basketball game doesn't seem so important now.

What made the game important at the time? The answer is simple: misplaced priorities. It is so easy to trade what is truly important for what we want at the moment. Basketball was something I wanted to do at the moment, and I reasoned that it was a lot more appealing than going to the hospital yet again. So I procrastinated, thinking that I would just meet Arlene at the hospital later. Thus, I missed the opportunity to fulfill my responsibilities.

The answer to this kind of dilemma is simplified by considering the covenants made in the temple. There is no way I could, nor would I want to, delegate my covenants with my wife and son to someone else. That is one of the reasons we make sacred covenants in the temples, to remind us to whom our responsibilities lie.

I have learned that you can delegate authority but you cannot delegate responsibility. I had tried to delegate my responsibility to a neighbor, thinking that transportation was the only issue involved. In truth, it was more important that I stop the game and send the boys home or bring in another adult to play basketball with them. In doing this, I would have appropriately delegated my authority as a teacher and at the same time maintained my responsibility to my family. There can be substitute teachers, but there can be no substitute husbands and fathers. In my own way, I had misplaced my priorities to a greater degree than the social worker or the other people who had felt that they had let our family down.

I recall a popular movie in which a teacher had his young male students stand in front of one of the walls in the hallway of the school, which pictured many former students who had attended the school long before. The young men in the pictures, who appeared so full of life, were now old or even dead; their time for being students had come and gone. The teacher stood behind the newest generation of students, who were gazing toward the past, and whispered, "Carpe diem," which is Latin for "Seize the day." The message was simple yet profound: Do it now.

Of course, this thought is not original. Amulek placed it in an eternal perspective when he counseled the Zoramites in the Book of Mormon: "If we do not improve our time while in this life, then cometh the night of darkness wherein there can be no labor performed" (Alma 34:33).

Boyd's passing and the events that came after it were filled with so much to learn. The lesson regarding procrastination was one I did not want to forget.

11

MOVING FORWARD

I n the days following Boyd's passing and preceding the funeral, our home was like a beehive swarming with activity. We were overwhelmed by the support of friends and loved ones. And the flowers—what beautiful flowers! Boyd loved flowers, and I'm sure he would have spent much time looking at each arrangement delivered to our door.

However, the excitement didn't keep us from wondering how all this would affect Boyd's brothers. When we visited with the doctors following Boyd's death, we were told that the first order of business was to sit down with our children and tell them that his passing was not their fault. We were advised that in death, divorce, and other family tragedies children tend to blame themselves, and the effects of this on their own lives can be far-reaching. We followed instructions with what seemed to be successful results. It is difficult to know what is right in such a situation. We did the best we could under the circumstances and tried to trust in the Lord.

Spencer was less than two years old, so we were confident he would be able to accept Boyd's passing with a minimal amount of emotional and psychological trauma. He would learn to understand it better as he grew older. The fact that Spencer had cystic fibrosis placed us in a position to have to follow up with him much differently than we would with Preston.

We were concerned about Preston's ability to cope with the loss of his older brother and best friend. Preston had always been close to Boyd, but in the last few weeks of Boyd's life, they had become inseparable. Toward the end of his life, Boyd even wanted Preston to sleep with him. As Preston noticed Boyd's dependency on others, he became his guardian—making sure he had a cup of water during coughing spells, patting Boyd on the back when he had to throw up, and always making sure Boyd had his favorite blanket. We just didn't know how he would deal with the situation.

We recalled Preston's inability to accept the death of the little kitten. Would he block this out of his mind in the same way? We tried to keep our attitude positive as we told him of Boyd's passing. He accepted all that we said without saying much and went back out to play. Arlene and I looked at each other and agreed we would have to wait and see what developed.

A day before Boyd's funeral, a family came by to offer their condolences. Arlene and I were in the back of the house, so they waited on the couch in the front room. Preston pulled the footstool in front of them and sat down.

He said solemnly, "Did you hear what happened to my best friend, Boyd? He died and is now living with Heavenly

Father." This was the first thing Preston had said that gave us any indication that he was grasping the situation.

We were also concerned about how Preston might react when he saw Boyd's body before the funeral. We debated whether to let him see Boyd again, but with some reservations, we agreed it would be for the best.

The day of the funeral, we took Preston and Spencer into the viewing room before anyone else arrived. I asked Preston to walk over and touch Boyd's hand.

"It doesn't feel like Boyd, does it, son?" I asked. He was a bit surprised that it didn't. "Boyd's spirit has left his body and is now living with Heavenly Father. That is why his body feels so different—his spirit isn't in it anymore. This is called death. In a little while, Heavenly Father is going to give Boyd his body again in its perfect state. This is called a resurrected body, and it will not give him pain anymore. His spirit will be able to live in his resurrected body forever. I'm sure Boyd misses us like we miss him, but he is very happy. Eventually we will all live with Boyd again in heaven." This was not the first time we had had this discussion; we had reviewed this topic as a family a number of times.

Shortly after our conversation, Preston proved himself to be quite a missionary. A lady entered the viewing room and walked by the casket to look at Boyd's body. She became overwhelmed with emotion and sat down in one of the chairs nearby. Preston walked over to her and said, "Don't cry. Boyd is with Heavenly Father, and he's happy. His body over there in that box quit working, so he has gone back to Heavenly Father to get a new one. Someday our whole family is going to live with Boyd again."

As I stood in the background listening, I was comforted

by Preston's speech. In time he would better understand that getting a new body does not mean that our mortal bodies are rejected in favor of a totally unrelated resurrected tabernacle. Preston had more basic needs at this point.

I wish to interject something at this point that may be of value to families who may be going through similar situations as ours. As the years progressed, our wonderful son Preston struggled a bit, especially during his teens. My wife and I have pondered the degree to which Preston's struggles are connected to losing his older brother at such a tender time in his life. What a challenge it must have been for him in his early youth to have both his older and younger brothers afflicted with CF. Recently I came across an essay Preston wrote in high school, which is quite illuminating. There are elements in his writing that indicate some unfinished business regarding his brother's passing. I share it in the hope that if parents have lost a child to death, that they take time to ensure that each child remaining in the home is able to make a healthy transition toward recovery in the future. I share this with Preston's approval. It is titled "Soda Pop":

> As I think back on my childhood, I think of it in stages. One of the stages was in Phoenix, Arizona, at the age of six. I still remember our house. In the front yard there were two big trees with a chain-link fence. The road was big, with five lanes and never-ending cars. The front yard was off-limits to any kid. No one went into the front yard, unless with parents.
>
> The backyard was different, though. Every corner was filled with memories and make-believe. Since we couldn't go in the front yard, my parents and the next-door neighbors' parents took down the fence separating our [back] yards. So a little boy named Brandon next door and I were

free to roam back and forth.

Brandon was always playing make-believe, to the extent that he never told the truth. We would tell each other make-believe stories. . . .

To the side of my house there was a clubhouse. In the back was a tree house with a trampoline underneath. In the other yard there was a sandbox under a big tree. At the far end of the yard there was the biggest swing set ever. It seemed to tower over everything. This swing set upon command would turn into a pirate ship or just a circus.

I had just lost my older brother Boyd to the disease cystic fibrosis. I lost my best friend when he died. Even though I was young, I was very perceptive. I was sad and at the same time mad at God for taking my brother and my best friend.

When my brother died it hurt me so much I simply denied he was dead to the extent that I insisted he was sleeping in his coffin and tried to climb in and wake him up. I almost tipped the coffin over. Later I went on to forget that I ever knew or had an older brother and to deny his existence. What bothered me more than anything was that I had a younger brother that had the same disease that Boyd died of. I was afraid of death, not only the death of myself, but also the death of another and being left all alone.

Death was constantly on my mind. I had this recurring nightmare every night. It would start out that I was in my bed at night. I would feel very hot, so I would kick off my covers and then toss and turn till I was sure I could not sleep. I would then get up. Immediately, I would feel something beckoning me. I would walk into the adjoining hall, then into the living room. I could hear the voice; it was outside. I would unlatch the dead bolt and open the front door. The voice was louder than ever, yet still a deathly cold whisper. I would walk out to the grass, then almost reaching a tree where the sound was the loudest, before I reached the tree, a big cold mass of blackness in the form of a man would swoop out from behind the tree and grab me. Consumed in utter cold darkness, I would wake up with a start in a sweat. I would never yell for my parents because I knew that if they couldn't have saved my brother from death, they could not save me.

I once had a German Shepherd puppy that was given to me by my friend's parents. I loved that puppy more than anything I knew. I was in the backyard playing with it once, and it was jumping around, and I was holding its back legs and playing with it kind of roughly. My dad saw me and said, "If you aren't careful you will kill that puppy." I didn't know what to think, but I knew I didn't want to have anything to do with a puppy that I would get attached to and would someday die and leave me. After that, I insisted that we get rid of the dog. After much talking, my parents agreed and gave it away.

Behind our yards there was an alley. The alley was big enough for a car or truck to drive down it. The alley was not to be entered. But whenever Brandon, me, or the black kid down the street named Rocky got money, we would sneak out when no one was looking and run down to Seven Eleven to get candy. . . .

The city was dangerous. Something that in any other place would be strange happened every day there. Everything from getting shot at with a pellet gun to getting our house burglarized and car stolen at night while we were asleep.

On this day, I woke up not being able to sleep any longer due to the hot sun coming through the window. I came out of the back sliding-glass door in our house. I went next door to see Brandon. I expected to see him watching Sesame Street or playing with his toys. Instead no one was home. Rocky wasn't over yet, so I went to the swing set and looked over the short chain-link fence. Over that fence was no-man's-land.

The house there was cracked, old, yellow stucco, and in the windows there were half-drawn curtains. On the windowsill there were little colored glass figures. The windows were very high and small. The backyard was covered with grass almost as high as the short fence, but white and dry. There was a shed in the back by the alley.

None of us had ever talked to the one person who lived there. He was an old man with gray hair. He never talked and rarely came into the yard. As I stared into the yard, I thought of all the stories Rocky, Brandon, and I always made up about why he was so secretive and how he buried kids in his backyard and that is why the grass grew so high, thriving off the decaying corpses.

Suddenly, I saw someone coming from around the far side of the house. It was him. I watched as he looked around and then looked at me. He started walking in my direction. I wanted to run, but I didn't. There was something in the way he looked that almost looked like he was nice.

He walked through the high grass in my direction. As the dry grass cracked under his feet, I thought if he talks his voice will probably be crackly and mean. About then, he reached the fence.

Then he talked to me. His voice sounded normal, not crackly and dry as I expected. He said, "Hi, what is your name." I told him that it was James [Preston's middle name]. Then, he asked me if I wanted a job. I thought for a second and then asked what kind of job. He said it would be in the backyard stacking shingles.

I thought, well it is in the backyard, so I won't have to go into his house. I slowly answered yes and then started to the back fence to walk through the alley to his house. I glanced around, looking for my mom to make sure she was not looking; then I went through the gate.

As I walked, I thought now I am going to be killed and buried in his backyard, but if I run he will hunt me down. But when I got into his yard he showed me the shingles, and he told me to stack them around the corner. I couldn't figure out why he wanted me to do this because it wasn't very hard. He probably had his reasons. As I picked some shingles up from one stack and walked around the corner, I saw the old man setting out two lawn chairs in the shade of the carport.

I thought of how when Brandon got home and Rocky came over we could sneak down the alley with the money I was going to make. I was going to buy everyone some candy. We would all probably get Bazooka bubble gum; at least that is what we usually got.

I finished then and turned towards the house. He was sitting there in the shade of the carport with two lawn chairs and a soda pop. I started to walk over to him to collect my pay when he said, "You have worked hard so go ahead and sit down." I sat down in the shade. He inquired, "You have worked, now what is your favorite soda pop?" I answered, "I like orange soda pop." He nodded and walked into the house and came back out and handed me a cold orange soda pop.

I was a pretty straightforward little kid, so I asked if he had a family. He answered, "No, my family is gone." I asked where they had gone. In a more serious tone with a very serious expression on his face, he said, "I had a wife and a son. My wife died a few years ago, but my son died when he was a little younger than you. He was at home one day with his mother when he crawled into the drying machine. He had fallen asleep in the dryer with all of the clothes when my wife closed the door as she went by. It turned on the dryer and my son was dead when she found him." He then said that I reminded him of his son.

He stared back into the alley. I stared there not knowing what to say. I no longer felt threatened by him. My soda pop was about gone by now. I heard my mom call my name. I got up and gave him my empty can as I said,

"That is my mom calling, I had better go now." He asked me if I could come back the next day. I told him I could. I then ran out of the gate, through the alley and back to my house.

When I told Rocky and Brandon what had happened, they couldn't believe I went there. I told them that he was nice, but they did not believe me. Whenever he would come ask me to do some work for him, they couldn't see why I went.

He died a year later, but he is probably happy now with his family. The house went abandoned and empty. He taught me a very valuable lesson: To never label people because of what other people tell you and how they look, and if you always think about death, you will forget to live. We moved away, the nightmares have stopped.

With 20/20 hindsight, I can see that we could have done more to help Preston with this transition. For many years, we were not aware of the struggles he was going through after the death of his brother. I would invite anyone who has had a situation similar to ours to seek out competent counselors to aid all the family members in their recovery, especially the siblings.

Preston's experience brings to mind an Easter story about an eleven-year-old boy with Down's syndrome named Philip and his Sunday School class. Elder Marion D. Hanks shared this experience in general conference:

> Easter Sunday the teacher brought an empty plastic egg for each child. They were instructed to go out of the church building onto the grounds and put into the egg something that would remind them of the meaning of Easter.
>
> All returned joyfully. As each egg was opened there were exclamations of delight at a butterfly, a twig, a flower,

a blade of grass. Then the last egg was opened. It was Philip's, and it was empty!

Some of the children made fun of Philip. "But, teacher," he said, "teacher, the tomb was empty."

A newspaper article announcing Philip's death a few months later noted that at the conclusion of the funeral eight children marched forward and put a large empty egg on the small casket. On it was a banner that said, "The tomb was empty." ("The Royal Law," *Ensign,* May 1992, 11)

We have discovered the necessity of making sure, in a situation like the passing of Boyd, that all of the remaining siblings understand this concept of the "empty tomb."

I have learned something else that may be helpful to others following the death of a loved one. Immediately after the death of a family member, the family is often tempted to quickly move to a new area where they will not have haunting reminders. My experience would indicate that this might prove to be a faulty decision because family members lose the support structure of the very people who can help them through their recovery. Neighbors, ward members, and so many others who were there during Boyd's final hours were an unexpected source of strength in the recovery process.

Individuals who have lost a loved one and then immediately moved away will not feel comfortable striking up a conversation about what they are going through with people who did not even know the deceased or weren't there in the final chapters of his life. Even if they are moving so that they can be close to other family members, there are so many other changes that they initiate by moving, such as a new job and new ward, as well as new neighbors and friends. All of these and many other changes may add more to a sense of loss than to feelings of recovery. The echoes of familiar objects and places near home that are so difficult immediately following a death may eventually become a great comfort, create a feeling of warmth, and be a familiar reminder of the loved one we have lost.

We need not be too quick to rearrange or redecorate the house in an effort to avoid the painful reminders of our loss. Time heals, and the people who have patience, who are not running from their feelings, will redecorate or relocate for more appropriate and long-lasting reasons than just trying to escape the pain. At the opposite end of the spectrum, which is just as harmful, is the person who never enters the deceased person's bedroom or, worse yet, turns it into a kind of museum where the living can look but never touch.

Quite often a quick change of locations becomes most damaging to the children. Not only have they lost a loved one, but now they have also lost their school, neighborhood, church, and many of the people surrounding them, all of which have defined them up to this point. Sometimes change is good, but parents need to consider that major changes immediately following the death of a family member can be especially hard on children. (This is a general observation rather than specific counsel.)

I share these observations, having learned from my own mistakes, as well as from observing others who have traveled through the same mourning process. While each of us will spend a moment or two in life traveling through a darkened tunnel, it would be foolish for us, during these times, to plan our future as if we were going to live the rest of our lives in a tunnel. We will eventually travel through the darkness into the light, where we can then make our long-range plans.

The analogy of the tunnel is drawn from the engulfment a person may experience immediately following the death of a loved one. But the shadow of death, like the darkness of the tunnel, will pass. We must make our life changes or alterations in the light. Time heals, and this too will pass. It is a fact of life—a reality that none of us can escape—that we bury those we love until those we love bury us.

We must travel carefully through those periods of life and recognize that drastic changes in our lives immediately following the death of a loved one may contribute more to the problem than to the solution. I recognize that some of the quick changes we made following Boyd's death were inspired more by the need to run from the pain than anything else. I think this made the recovery process a little harder on Preston than it needed to be.

12

JOURNAL WRITING

President Spencer W. Kimball said, "Your own private journal should record the way you face up to challenges that beset you. Do not suppose life changes so much that your experiences will not be interesting to your posterity. . . . What could you do better for your children and your children's children than to record the story of your life, your triumphs over adversity, your recovery after a fall, your progress when all seemed black, your rejoicing when you had finally achieved? . . . A journal will last through all time, and maybe the angels may quote from it for eternity. ... Remember, the Savior chastised those who failed to record important events" (*Teachings of Spencer W. Kimball,* ed. Edward L. Kimball [Salt Lake City: Bookcraft, 1982], 350–51).

Arlene kept a journal for each of our older children from their birth. Quite often she arose early in the morning to write in their journals or organize pictorial histories of our

family for the past year. When these children became respon-
sible enough to continue their own journal, this task was
passed on to them.

What a blessing this has been for me—my recovery after
Boyd's passing has been aided by reading Arlene's, Boyd's,
and my own journal, kept during the six years that Boyd lived
with us. Preston's writings have aided me in understanding his
feelings regarding the loss of his older brother. Time would
have erased all of the sweet memories and might have left a
residue of pain and even bitterness had I not been able to keep
perspective through the occasional use of these journals.

Following the viewing of our son's body, we stepped into
the chapel for the funeral. During the funeral, I'm sure everyone's heart was touched when our friend Widtsoe Shumway
used Boyd's journal as the text for his talk. (Boyd had dictated
much of the journal to Arlene.) In a sense, Boyd spoke at his
own funeral through his journal.

I mention the journal reading at the funeral to point out
an important occurrence. The chapel in which the funeral was
held was also a part of the building in which I taught seminary. It was located next to Arcadia High School in Phoenix.
Only a small proportion of the student body was composed of
members of The Church of Jesus Christ of Latter-day Saints,
but the nonmember principal paid tribute to their influence
by excusing all of the students from the high school to attend
the funeral.

For weeks following this event, young people who had
heard the gospel for the first time at the funeral trickled over
to my office and inquired about the Church. A few said they
felt something they had never felt before. Of course, members of the Church recognize that "something" as the Holy

Ghost, which was present at the proceedings. From seeds planted at the funeral, two students were taught and baptized. It is fascinating how the Lord uses times like these to touch hearts. Boyd went through the process of being physically taken home to his God, while two of our Heavenly Father's children began the process of spiritually coming home.

Many years later, while I was teaching at Brigham Young University, a student asked me, "Are you the Brother Bassett who taught seminary in Phoenix, Arizona?"

Following my affirmative response, he indicated that he was one of the nonmember students from the high school who had been there at Boyd's funeral. At the same time, he was being fellowshipped by some wonderful LDS friends and even visited seminary a few times. He announced to me that he had been baptized later and had served a full-time mission. His reason for approaching me was to let me know that he was going to be sealed to his sweetheart in the temple in a few weeks and that he wished to invite me to the reception. I think it is amazing that the Lord uses such events as death and funerals to initiate life and new beginnings for others. This young man was living proof. I am so grateful that my wife kept a journal for Boyd so that, even after his passing, his words could plant a seed in this young man's heart. Then, with the help of some of the great seminary students at Arcadia High School, this seed was nourished and eventually brought forth fruit.

After the funeral, we watched the pallbearers place the casket inside the hearse. I can't recall ever feeling so helpless. Even though we knew that it was only Boyd's mortal body inside that box, we could not feel comfortable until our son's body was properly buried in Utah.

We drove home and quietly changed our clothes. How fortunate we were to be surrounded by so many friends and family in the days following Boyd's death. What a shield they were against the pain. Even with them, there were moments when his loss came crashing home.

Shortly after his passing, Arlene went to the store to buy groceries for the family. Her journal entry regarding this event illustrates the power of keeping a journal of life's events and feelings.

> After Boyd's death, funeral, and burial, family members had filled many of my normal routines. I hadn't shopped for groceries for about a week and a half. Since Boyd's death, I felt everything I did during the day was done by remote control. My mind was literally telling my body step-by-step how to function, one command at a time: "Get dressed, brush teeth, get baby up, change diapers . . . etc." This morning I had prepared both Preston and Spencer for a trip to the grocery store. I got into the car and drove the five miles. As I was walking through the aisles of the store, I was congratulating myself on this uneventful trip. I was moving forward in spite of not wanting to. Shortly after this thought, I turned into the cereal aisle. The first cereal box my eyes focused on was one that Boyd had asked for several times—one he had seen on cartoon commercials. The uneventful trip was over. I searched for a quiet corner of the store to cry. It seemed almost foolish now that I had countered every [one of Boyd's] demand[s] with the wisdom that they weren't good for him and therefore we couldn't buy them. Now, how I wished that I could buy them and see his joyous face receive just such a surprise."

With Boyd's passing, I could certainly understand why President Spencer W. Kimball said that the word *remember* could be considered "the most important word" in the dictionary ("Circles of Exaltation," in *Charge to Religious Educators* [Salt Lake City: The Church of Jesus Christ of Latter-day Saints, 1981], 12). For a season after his death, it seemed that all the small and simple things in our surroundings—like cereal boxes—brought memories of him echoing into our hearts. I have learned that having recorded the events of Boyd's life has directly connected us to this remembering process, especially for his younger brothers and sisters born since his passing.

I am convinced that journal writing gives each of us the opportunity to speak from the dust and continue to make a difference in the lives of people here in mortality. Our words may be a deciding factor in saving the soul of one of our own relatives who may get to know us only through our journal because they were born after we passed away. Perhaps this is what President Kimball meant when he said "angels may quote from it for eternity" ("The Angels May Quote from It," *New Era,* October 1975, 5). Perhaps we will be one of those angels who speak through the veil to our loved ones reading our journals. In a very real sense, when we die, our voice is silenced to those left in mortality—if we do not keep a record of our lives.

Let me illustrate how just a little effort can make a tremendous difference in the lives of those we love. In chapter 4 I mentioned that my father passed away around the time Preston was born. Dad had known for quite some time that his days were numbered. On one evening, while my mother was at work and with the house all to himself, he did something that illustrated his great love for my mom.

He brought out the tape recorder and recorded his most tender feelings for my mother. In a sense, he recorded a love letter to his wife—sharing his emotion and devotion for her at the conclusion of his life. He then hid the tape behind some books on the bookshelf, expecting that this small treasure would be discovered following his death.

My mom is a *cleanaholic.* My dad knew that she would eventually dust the bookshelves and discover the tape. In this way, he could literally speak from the dust to his wife—offering her words of love, comfort, and encouragement to carry on without him.

Shortly after his funeral, Mom was busily cleaning the house and happened to come across this tape. Imagine her feelings upon placing it in the tape player and hearing her recently departed companion expressing his love and appreciation to her for the life they had spent together. That tape has become an important part of our family history.

What little effort it took on my father's part to record his feelings on that tape—maybe five minutes out of his life—yet its value cannot be measured in terms of money; it is truly priceless to our family. Each of us has the opportunity to keep a record of our feelings and testimonies, which could be a lifeline that may touch, inspire, or direct a loved one after we have passed through the veil (see Appendix, 190). This becomes one of the ways we participate in the mission of Elijah, which is to bind the hearts of the fathers to the children.

13

PACE AND PRIORITIES

Elder Melvin J. Ballard wrote, "I lost a son six years of age and *I saw him a man in the spirit world after his death,* and I saw how he had exercised his own freedom of choice and would obtain of his own will and volition a companionship, and in due time to him and all those who are worthy of it, shall come all of the blessings and sealing privileges of the house of the Lord" (*Three Degrees of Glory* [Salt Lake City: Magazine Printing Co., 1955], 40–41).

The day after the funeral, we had Boyd's body flown from Phoenix to Salt Lake City, where he was to be buried next to Arlene's mother. As we drove to the cemetery for Boyd's burial the clouds that had covered the city for several days opened and allowed the sun to warm this occasion. We were deeply touched by the number of people in attendance. The reverent circumstances of Boyd's burial served as a warm reunion for friends and family. There were people whom we hadn't seen since our days in college. It is sad that it takes events such as this to bring us together with the ones we dearly love.

After the burial ceremony, Arlene's family took us to dinner at a comfortable restaurant on the east side of Salt Lake City. A small room was reserved for our meal. I was seated at the head of a table large enough to accommodate the entire group.

My brother-in-law David Howells was seated to my right at the corner of the table. David is hard of hearing and must wear a hearing aid in each ear. This causes sounds to become muffled and difficult to distinguish when he is in a group of people. He is a wonderful man who lives close to the Spirit. My life has been blessed by priesthood blessings received at his hands. As long as I dwell in mortality, I will be enriched by an experience he had during our meal.

Most of us were conversing somewhat lightheartedly when Dave put his hand on my arm, leaned over, and whispered in my ear, "Remind me to tell you what just happened."

As he sat back in his chair, I noticed his eyes were filled with tears and he was struggling with his emotions. Later in the evening, when everything had settled down, he related to me what had happened: "As we were sitting at the table enjoying each other's company, I heard a voice say loudly and abruptly, 'Boyd!' Thinking you may have said it, Doug, I looked at you. I then looked at everyone else at the table. I thought it strange that even with my hearing problem I was apparently the only one to hear it. I then looked back at you. Then I saw him—Boyd was standing in spirit to your left about ten feet away, just across the table from me. He was tall and had beautiful blonde hair. He was a mature spirit, not yet in his resurrected body. He was not a little boy but appeared to be a young man in his full stature. Boyd was smiling and seemed to be very happy. There is no doubt in my mind that this young man was Boyd."

Following David's remarks, my first thought was, "How could a boy who died at age six appear in his full stature?" President Joseph F. Smith wrote: "If you see one of your children that has passed away it may appear to you in the form in which you would recognize it, the form of childhood; *but if it came to you as a messenger bearing some important truth, it would perhaps come . . . in the stature of full-grown manhood. . . .* The spirit of Jesus was full-grown before He was born into the world; and so our children were full-grown and possessed their full stature in the spirit before they entered mortality" (*Improvement Era,* February 1918, 570–71; emphasis added).

I felt that David's experience was true because the Spirit was present. Boyd's appearance mirrored the words of Elder Dallin H. Oaks: "Many, including some in my extended family, have seen a departed loved one in vision or personal appearance and have witnessed their restoration in 'proper and perfect frame' (Alma 40:23) in the prime of life. Whether these were manifestations of persons already resurrected or of righteous spirits awaiting an assured resurrection, the reality and nature of the resurrection of mortals is evident. What a comfort to know that all who have been disadvantaged in life from birth defects . . . will be resurrected in 'proper and perfect frame'" ("Resurrection," *Ensign,* May 2000, 15).

Boyd's appearance was consistent with the spiritual support the Lord had blessed us with throughout the last week of his life—the little bird, which had provided such a wonderful teaching moment for Boyd and Preston, the experience at the hospital with the two LDS doctors replacing the one who had been there for two years, the Lord answering our prayers concerning Boyd's last visit with the family, and the Spirit that provided comfort during Boyd's last hours on earth.

However, one question continued to haunt me. Why had *I* not seen Boyd? As the days passed, this began to weigh on me more and more.

With this question still on my mind, I was reading the Book of Mormon when my eyes fell upon what I believe was the answer. Jacob was preparing to teach the Nephites the allegory of Zenos. He stated, "I will unfold this mystery unto you; if I do not, by any means, get *shaken from my firmness in the Spirit, and stumble because of my over anxiety*" (Jacob 4:18; emphasis added).

I stopped and reviewed the circumstances once again. Here was a prophet, in the temple, preaching the doctrines of the kingdom, and he was concerned about losing the Spirit over something as simple as anxiety. Even the worthy prophet Jacob could not be sensitive to the promptings of the Spirit when anxiety was a part of his life.

I had grown up assuming that the companionship of the Spirit was the reward for the absence of sin; that not participating in drugs, alcohol, sexual sin, and so forth would allow the Spirit to permeate our lives. Jacob seemed to be suggesting that it takes more than reacting to the negative—we must also be proactive toward the Spirit, even in our attitude. Thus, the prophetic reminder to maintain a disposition that rises above something as simple as anxiety.

I thought back to the experience of David seeing my son while I was not in tune to the event. Because of David's hearing problem and general disposition, he was not caught up in the laughter and light-minded conversation taking place at the table. This placed him in a frame of mind and spirit to be in tune with Boyd's visit. I was completely caught up in the activities at the table and was so busy that my son Boyd could not make an impression on me. My way of coping with Boyd's death was to insulate myself from my pain by trying to make everyone laugh, while my own heart was filled with anxiety.

In the days that followed, I read further in the Book of Mormon. I came to King Benjamin's marvelous discourse to the Nephites in the latter stages of his life. His speech had given the audience much to digest in their already busy lives. He gave them a key to traveling through life at a pace that would allow the Spirit to be their companion: "And see that all these things are done in wisdom and order; for it is not requisite that a man should run faster than he has strength. And again, it is expedient that he should be diligent, that thereby he might win the prize; therefore, all things must be done in order" (Mosiah 4:27).

Notice the dynamics of what he is saying to the Nephites and to us. It is not enough to do what is right; we must also learn to conduct our lives at a pace that is diligent and, at the same time, does not cause us to "run faster than [we have] strength." There is a pace to living that allows the Lord to be our guide as we keep the commandments. I seemed to have been running at an internal pace that David was not.

It is ironic to me that while we may be able to answer honestly all of the temple recommend questions and be worthy to enter the temple, it is also true that the pace of our lives can keep us from the daily companionship of that Spirit we so desire. In Mosiah 4:27, King Benjamin encouraged each of us to run life's race with diligence. His words remind us that life's race is not a sprint but a long-distance race. Unlike a sprint, a long-distance race must be run at a pace that allows us to finish strong, or as the scriptures say, "endure [to] the end" (1 Nephi 13:37).

The Lord referred to this concept following the loss of the 116-page manuscript, when he counseled the Prophet Joseph Smith: "Do not run faster or labor more than you have strength" (D&C 10:4). "But," one might say, "what about the words of Spencer W. Kimball about lengthening our stride?" I would suggest that, even in a long distance race, the runner must lengthen his stride; he just doesn't do it so early in the race that he has no second wind—becoming exhausted so that he cannot endure to the end.

Words from the book of Hebrews echo this same theme: "Let us run with *patience* the race that is set before us" (Hebrews 21:1; emphasis added). Patience is not required in a sprint.

Perhaps a story related by President Harold B. Lee best illustrates this point of spiritual pace. His audience was the seminary and institute personnel for the Church:

> A few weeks ago, President McKay related to the Twelve an interesting experience. . . . He said it is a great thing to be responsive to the whisperings of the Spirit, and we know that when these whisperings come it is a gift and our privilege to have them. *They come when we are relaxed and not under pressure of appointments.* (I want you to mark that.) The President then took occasion to relate an experience in the life of Bishop John Wells, former member of the Presiding Bishopric.
>
> A son of Bishop Wells was killed in Emigration Canyon on a railroad track. . . . His boy was run over by a freight train. Sister Wells was inconsolable. She mourned

during the three days prior to the funeral, received no comfort at the funeral, and was in a rather serious state of mind.

One day soon after the funeral services while she was lying on her bed *relaxed,* still mourning, she said her son appeared to her and said, "Mother, do not mourn, do not cry. I am all right." He told her that she did not understand how the accident happened and explained that he had given the signal to the engineer to move on, and then made the usual effort to catch the railing on the freight train; but as he attempted to do so his foot caught on a root and he failed to catch the handrail, and his body fell under the train. It was clearly an accident.

Now listen. He said that as soon as he realized that he was in another environment he tried to see his father, *but couldn't reach him. His father was so busy with the duties in his office he could not respond to his call.* Therefore, he had come to his mother. He said to her, "You tell father that all is well with me, and I want you not to mourn anymore." (*The Teachings of Harold B. Lee,* ed. Clyde J. Williams [Salt Lake City: Bookcraft, 1996], 414–15; emphasis added)

As I read this story, I better understood the elements that prevented me from experiencing the visit of my son. Bishop Wells coped with the death of his son by going back to work. Even though this was the Lord's work, apparently this good man could not be reached by his departed son because of the *anxious* pace of his life. On the other hand, his wife was alone in the attitude of pondering and was able to be visited by her son.

Elder Boyd K. Packer said:

Too many of us are like those whom the Lord said ". . . were baptized with fire and with the Holy Ghost, *and they knew it not*" (3 Nephi 9:20). Imagine that: "And they knew it not." It is not unusual for one to have received the gift [of the Holy Ghost] and not really know it. I fear that this supernal gift is being obscured by programs and activities and schedules and so many meetings. There are so many places to go, so many things to do in this noisy world. We can be too busy to pay attention to the promptings of the Spirit. The voice of the Spirit is a still, small voice—a voice that is felt rather than heard. It is a spiritual voice that comes into the mind as a thought put into your heart. ("The Cloven Tongues of Fire," *Ensign,* May 2000, 8)

So why did I miss my son? Jacob suggests that "anxiety" or stress plays a part in spiritual communication. King Benjamin spoke of a spiritual pace that must be paid attention to as we run life's race. President Harold B. Lee reinforced this thesis with his story from the life of Bishop Wells. I believe that these are the reasons I did not participate in this event with my son. But understanding this has helped me in the time since my son's passing to ensure that I can be more in tune to the spiritual things happening around me.

It has been good for me to consider the words of Elder Henry B. Erying: "The still, small voice . . . is so quiet that if you are noisy inside, you won't hear it" (*To Draw Closer to God: A Collection of Discourses* [Salt Lake City: Deseret Book, 1997], 18). The anxiety I was experiencing caused me to be "noisy inside," which did not allow me to be edified by Boyd's appearance as was my brother-in-law. What a challenge—to learn how to give 100 percent of our energy and, at the same time, conduct ourselves at a pace at which we can feel the whisperings of the still, small voice. It is so easy to have an accelerated pace in life that leaves us busily trying to stay alive at the expense of experiencing and reflecting on the magnificent joy of simply being alive. On another occasion,

Elder Erying said, "Now, I testify it is a small voice. It whispers, not shouts" ("To Draw Closer to God," *Ensign*, May 1991, 67). I recognized that I needed to make some changes in my life.

I am reminded of the story of an elderly man who was resting by the side of a much-traveled path. A much younger man stopped for a minute next to the old gentleman. During the course of their conversation, the younger man asked, "How has life in America changed most?"

The old man replied simply, "Speed." After pausing for a moment to think, he continued. "It's killing us. You have to make a part of your life in which you slow down. The world won't do it for you."

It is like the song I sang so many years ago as a young boy: "Row, row, row your boat, gently down the stream. Merrily, merrily, merrily, merrily, life is but a dream." I heard Dr. Wayne Dyer teach that the word *gently* speaks to the pace of our life, while *merrily* reminds us of the attitude that the spiritually healthy give to themselves as a gift.

For me to recognize and respond to the promptings of the still small voice, I knew I needed to make a change in the pace of my life. The experience of Boyd's appearance brought home to me the reality of the words of George Q. Cannon: "If our eyes were open to see the spirit world around us, . . . we would not be so unguarded and careless and so indifferent whether we had the spirit and power of God with us or not but we would be continually watchful and prayerful to our Heavenly Father for His Holy Spirit and His holy angels to be around about us to strengthen us" (*Gospel Truth,* comp. Jerreld L. Newquist [Salt Lake City: Deseret News, 1987], 64–65).

An experience that happened many years after Boyd's death has relevance to the concept of spiritual pace.

It was the weekend before a new school year. I had all the feelings of anxiety and of running faster than I should as a teacher. For some reason, the days just before a new school year have always been a very stressful time for me. It is a feeling similar to those times when I was a young athlete, just before a contest was about to begin. It didn't matter what the sport was; the anxiety I felt just before the event was always the same. It always felt like a near-lethal mixture of anxiousness combined with fear and trembling.

On that particular day, this combination of emotions nearly became lethal for me as I was hurrying down the hallway just outside my classroom. As quickly as turning off a light switch, I suffered a heart attack that caused me to crumple to the floor. It was as if I had been unplugged from the power source that had kept me going for decades.

As my energy suddenly came to a halt, it seemed that the energy level of everyone in close proximity increased. With everything happening so fast around me, I felt like a spectator at an event that was of paramount importance to me but one in which I was not allowed to participate. I felt like a fish in an aquarium—watching others work all around me, yet I was unable to do anything except observe. My body had suddenly become so weak that it took all of my strength just to bring forth a whisper. Fearing that I might lose even that ability, I remained completely silent. Lying as still as possible, I placed my fate in the hands of trained professionals as well as the Lord.

It is amazing how the events of life change so quickly. One moment, I was walking down the hallway; the next,

I was waking up in a hospital bed a number of hours after a medical procedure that had required major anesthesia. All of this had taken almost a full day. How can something feel like it transpired in an instant *and* an eternity at the same time? The physical pace of my life had come to an abrupt halt. My "things to do" list had suddenly been wiped clean.

Still not knowing what had gone wrong with me physically, I awoke in great pain, accompanied by feelings of tremendous despair and anxiety. For some reason, there was nothing they could give me that would remove, or even dull, these monumental feelings.

This was early Sunday morning, and the doctor who had been working on me hustled into the room on his morning rounds. After a few minutes of conversation with my wife, he stepped toward the door. Almost as an afterthought, he turned to me and said, "Oh, you've had a heart attack. I'll be back later in the evening to discuss it with you."

A number of my relatives, including my father, had died very young of heart attacks or strokes. The doctor's words brought me to the shocking realization of my own mortality. As he walked through the doorway and moved briskly in the direction of the next item on his list of things to do, I interrupted his exit by appealing, "Can't we take a minute now and talk about this?"

He looked at me with eyes that seemed to have a firm focus on personal priorities. No longer referring to me as a patient but as a member of the Church, he said, "Brother Bassett, I am surprised at you. This is Sunday; you know that I am a bishop and that I have priesthood executive meeting this morning, as well as other council meetings, to attend to before sacrament meeting." Following this gentle chiding, he continued, "I'll see you later tonight." Without waiting for a reply, he exited the room.

As I lay there alone in the midst of my despair, my heart cried out, "Am I not more important than a meeting? Aren't people more important than meetings?"

Even in the midst of my self-pity, I was fully aware that my doctor was a good man and a dedicated bishop. He had no intention of hurting me; in fact, his only goal was to aid me in my recovery. His plate was just overflowing with people who needed his time professionally and ecclesiastically. He did not have the time to meet the needs of all the people who demanded his attention. Still, I felt there was a lesson for me to learn in the experience.

How I wished that I could go back and meet the needs of those I had unknowingly passed by because I had been running too fast to be sensitive to their needs. As I lay there in that bed, my mind raced back through the years to all those who had been in the position of need I was currently in—perhaps not physically but emotionally or spiritually, to be sure. But just as this doctor was unaware of my feelings at that time, I too was not aware of those I had dealt with in this manner. I had been so caught up in my own list of things to do that I wondered how many people, students, neighbors, and, perhaps, even family members had come to me in pain and despair and left with the feeling that a meeting, or someone else, or maybe just my own time, was more important to me than they were.

My frustration lay in the fact that I had been guilty of the same thing so many times and in so many positions of service over the years. I was reminded, once again, that quite often we don't see the world as it is; we see the world as we are. I had now come eye to eye with someone just like me, and I did not enjoy the view.

Elder Neal A. Maxwell wrote, "Imperviousness to the promptings of the still small voice of God will . . . mean that we have ears, but cannot hear, not only the promptings of God but also the pleas of men" (*A Time to Choose* [Salt Lake City: Deseret Book, 1972], 59–60, 71). As I lay in the hospital bed, I had time to ponder the pace of my own service, that it had been such that I too had not been as sensitive to "the promptings of the still small voice" and "the pleas of men" as I needed to be. And now this heart attack had suddenly wiped my planner clean, and I was left to ponder how I wanted to conduct myself when I got back on my feet. Certainly, my decision for the future was not to cancel or avoid all meetings but to use those meetings more profitably and not to schedule so many of them that the needs of the very people I was trying to serve became secondary. I made a commitment to myself that I would make every attempt to avoid getting so caught up in my activities, programs, and meetings that I might fail to respond to a suffering soul whose only need may be a listening ear (see Appendix, 191).

As I reviewed what had taken place, I realized that I had a choice. I could be angry, which would benefit no one, or I could learn and profit from this experience. Summoning all my limited energies, I willed to select the latter of the two choices. I never wanted to forget the feelings of need and dependence I had following my heart attack, and I recognized that if the Lord granted me the opportunity to serve again, there would be others who would approach me with that same kind of despair.

It is vitally important that we conduct our lives at a

spiritual pace that allows us to respond appropriately to the promptings of the Spirit. It is also of paramount importance to have our priorities in perspective. Pace must always be accompanied by priorities. And how can we be made constantly aware of these priorities? The answer is found in the covenants we have made, as well as in losing ourselves in the service of our fellowman. Although my heart attack took place many years after Boyd's death, it was a continuation of my learning experience that began when Boyd was born.

14

THE HEALING BALM OF SERVICE

A few days after Boyd's burial in Salt Lake City, we returned home to Phoenix. Three weeks of teaching remained before the school year ended. In the short time following Boyd's death, I was surprised at how well I was able to contain my emotions; the full weight of his passing had not really hit me—yet. In truth, my head had accepted his death, but my heart had not been completely acclimated to living without him. Now that I was home, I would be faced once again with the day-to-day reminders that he was gone.

A number of times toward the end of Boyd's life, he was just too weak to get up with me in the morning before I went to work. This troubled him a great deal, so he asked his mother to get him out of bed just as I was leaving to teach seminary. With Arlene's help, he would place his oxygen tank near the front window and peer out. He would then wave and blow me kisses as I warmed up the car. For me, the importance of this ritual was beyond measure.

On the first day back home, I sat warming up the car in the driveway before leaving for seminary. Without thinking, I found myself searching the window in the front of the house for Boyd's face. I looked for his hand waving and blowing kisses. Where was Boyd? It hit me instantly: "He's really gone!" The thought of living without him was too much for my heart to bear. I leaned against the steering wheel and wept until my soul was drained. The flow of tears seemed to be lubricating my heart for the tough times ahead. My heart was now coming to grips with what my head had accepted earlier.

The following words, which I did not write, came to my mind: "If my tears could build a stairway, my memories a lane, I would walk right up to heaven and bring you home again." I didn't know it was possible for a heart to ache as mine did at that moment and not break.

Before Boyd's death, if a person had approached Arlene and me to offer us four more hours in each waking day, he would have definitely had our attention. If he had also offered us an additional three hours of sleep each night, our interest would most certainly have been piqued. (These were the usual blocks of time that we had given to Boyd's cystic fibrosis over the major part of the past six years.) If this person were to further explain that the cost of these additional hours was to lose Boyd's little smiling face blowing kisses out the window, then the price would have been too great to pay.

In the week following Boyd's death, we had gained three to four more hours in each day. We were also sleeping all night for the first time in years. Yet, the price we had paid for this extra time was a great burden to bear. The extra hours in each day only gave us more time to ponder our loss. In a way, death itself was not as difficult to deal with as learning how to carry on without his smiling face blowing kisses out the window. We were forced to face the reality that, in some ways, we had to lock his memory away in our hearts until we could feel, touch, and love him face-to-face once again.

At this point in my life, I could relate more than ever to the deep expressions of President Joseph F. Smith upon losing his precious three-year-old daughter, Mercy Josephine, whom he called "Dodo." He wrote these words in a letter to his wife Edna:

> I scarce dare to trust myself to write, even now my heart aches, and my mind is all chaos; if I should murmur, may God forgive me, my soul has been and is tried with poignant grief, my heart is bruised and wrenched almost asunder. I am desolate, my home seems desolate and almost dreary . . . my own sweet Dodo is gone! I can scarcely believe it and my heart asks, Can it be? I look in vain, I listen, no sound, I wander through the rooms, all are vacant, lonely, desolate, deserted. I look down the garden walk, peer around the house, look here and there for a glimpse of a little golden, sunny head and rosy cheeks, but no, alas, no pattering little footsteps. No beaming little black eyes sparkling with love for papa; no sweet little inquiring voice . . . no soft dimpled hands clasping me around the neck, no sweet rosy lips returning in childish innocence my fond embrace and kisses, but a vacant little chair. Her little toys are concealed, her clothes put by, and only the one desolate thought forcing its crushing leaden weight upon my heart—she is not here, she is gone! . . . I am almost wild, and O God only knows how much I loved my girl, and she the light and joy of my heart." ("Families and Generational Gaps," *The New Era,* January 1972, 43)

There have been tears and there will be more, but through

it all, we can't help thanking a loving Heavenly Father who let us borrow one of his children for six years. I am comforted by God's promise that, if we live worthily, we will have him again—this time forever. Boyd's mortal experience, his complete story, is not an account of death but an affirmation of life—eternal life!

More than 130 years ago in the Salt Lake Tabernacle, President Brigham Young said, "I have neither wife nor child, . . . they are only committed to me, to see how I will treat them. If I am faithful, the time will come when they will be given to me" (in *Journal of Discourses,* 26 vols. [London: Latter-day Saints' Book Depot, 1854–86], 10:298).

Before Boyd's passing, I understood this doctrine and had taught it many times, but in losing a loved one so dear to my heart, I was forced to fully appreciate it. For the season following Boyd's death, it was the hope I chose to cling to as I pressed on with my life here in mortality.

The gospel taught me how to find my son again, but the question still remained: How do I find myself, when the little boy I was tied so closely to was no longer with me? The following experience helped define the process for me.

A month after the death of our little six-year-old, I was transferred to Redding, California, to teach seminary. The rest of the family remained in Phoenix while I traveled west to find a home for us.

Without the loving arms of my family and friends, I found that the impact of losing Boyd increased profoundly in California. Now, instead of being surrounded by loved ones, I was engulfed in free time. There were still three months before school began. This gave me the opportunity to ponder my loss to the point of feeling sorry for myself. Unconsciously,

I even began to feel a bit forsaken by my God.

It has been said that a person all wrapped up in himself makes a pretty small package. I knew that this was happening to me. I realized that I must get immersed in an activity that would allow my broken life to mend. With this thought in mind, I knelt and pleaded with the Lord to help me structure my life again. I needed something worthwhile to fill my time.

The next morning the doorbell rang and, to my surprise, standing there in the doorway was a six-foot-one-inch answer to my prayer. He said, "Hello. My name is Mike McGee. Are you the new seminary teacher?"

Following my affirmative answer, he continued, "My father said that you used to be a coach. I would like to try out for the basketball team at school, and I was wondering if you could help me."

I must admit, I saw Mike initially as more of an opportunity to throw my efforts into a worthwhile venture than as a basketball player. I said yes to his request without really considering the actual possibility of his making the team. Fortunately, he was blessed with basic skills as well as a fighting heart that hungered to reach the goal.

Nevertheless, his request proved to be a real challenge because of the circumstances involved. This was to be his senior year, and he had never played on a school basketball team. To make it a little harder, the team he was trying out for had won the league championship the year before and had a core of starters returning. The Lord had really given me a task to get immersed in!

We met each morning at the church gym at 5:30 and practiced for two hours. We met again in the afternoon for two more hours of basketball. In addition to this, I gave Mike an extensive weight-lifting program. Through the rest of the summer, we worked with one goal in mind: for Mike to make the Shasta High School varsity basketball team! This was the perfect mental and physical outlet to keep me off the road to self-pity I had been on before I met Mike. The summer passed quickly, and my family and I were reunited in our new home. When the school year started, my responsibilities extended beyond the life of this one student. Still, the mark of excellence for the summer was to be determined during the tryouts for varsity basketball.

True to his goal, Mike burst on the scene with a vengeance. He not only made the team but also became a starter. With a lot of hard work, he had made his dream come true! I'm sure he learned more than just basketball in that summer of 1981. He set goals and worked hard, lessons that would serve him well as a missionary and future husband and father. Years later, I had the opportunity of being his teacher in a returned missionary Book of Mormon class at Brigham Young University. That wonderful quality of grit and not giving in to the odds, while still being aware of the costs that needed to be paid to reach a goal, were still a part of his character.

The time I spent with Mike reinforced for me the idea that to ease another's burdens serves to make your own a bit lighter. That season of service for me was also a season of healing. Of course, that idea is not original; the Savior said it best many centuries before in Galilee: "He that loseth his life for my sake shall find it" (Matthew 10:39; see Appendix, 194).

I have learned that it is important to have a balance between taking time to mourn following the death of a loved one and immersing ourselves in appropriate activities. Those who sit around over an extended period of time and mourn to the exclusion of daily living, place themselves in a dark hole where the Spirit of the Lord is not likely to visit. On the other hand, those who insulate themselves with activity, work, and service to separate themselves from necessary mourning may discover that the healing power of the Holy Ghost may not be their companion either. What a challenge it is to deal with life's constant changes and still maintain proper balance. My association with Mike brought a balance back into my life by allowing me to mourn for Boyd and, at the same time, lend service to another. This helped me to move forward at a comfortable pace without turning my back on my immediate loss.

15

MY WILL, THY WILL

I have come to understand that the way the Lord has dealt with us during and following Boyd's life has had much to do with our attitude in this process. Elder Dennis B. Neuenschwander said, "Whatever happens in the life of a person, *if his attitude is right,* the Lord will work that experience for that person's good" (faculty in-service, Orem Institute of Religion, December 14, 1996; emphasis added).

We can better understand this "attitude" spoken of by Elder Neuenschwander by viewing a contrast between two opposing attitudes in working with our Heavenly Father: The "my will," which is a self-desired view of the world, and the "thy will," or the desire of a person to understand and follow God's will during times of trial and adversity. This my will-thy will comparison is meant not as a categorization of people but as a description of attitudes that all of us have from time to time, depending on our spiritual perspective.

People who work with the Lord using a "my will" agenda in addressing life's challenges may view life's adversities, trials, or tragedies as if the painful obstacle before them is an insurmountable wall that God is to remove from their path. In a "my will" approach to prayer, Heavenly Father is viewed as a kind of spiritual Santa Claus. Just as Saint Nick is called upon only in one particular season each year, a person with a "my will" attitude approaches God only in a season of affliction. Once the trial has passed, the individual carries on with life, approaching God again when the seemingly insurmountable wall of adversity looms once again in his path.

Many children believe that at each yuletide season, the ticket for receiving Santa Claus's best gifts is to sit on his lap and say, "I've been good." Santa Claus gives his gifts based on an assessment of whether a child has been "naughty" or "nice." The "my will" approach to opposition assumes that the individual's role is to keep the commandments, and God's gift for those who have been obedient—or "nice," in Santa Claus terminology—is simply to make adversity go away.

When taken to the extreme, this spiritually warped view assumes that a spiritual Santa Claus's greatest gifts are health, wealth, worldly success, business security, and the total acceptance and appreciation of those around them. If this were true, then such people as Jesus Christ and Joseph Smith received few blessings from their Father in Heaven.

President Ezra Taft Benson referred to this self-centered agenda, saying, "We pit our will against God's. When we direct our pride toward God, it is in the spirit of *my will and not thine be done*. . . . The proud wish God would agree with them" ("Beware of Pride," *Ensign,* May 1989, 4; emphasis added).

On the same subject, Elder Erastus Snow said, "If our spirits are inclined to be stiff and refractory, and we desire continually the gratification of our own will to the extent that this feeling prevails in us, the Spirit of the Lord is held at a distance from us: or, in other words, *the Father withholds his Spirit from us in proportion as we desire the gratification of our own will*" (in *Journal of Discourses,* 26 vols. [London: Latter-day Saints' Book Depot, 1854–86], 7:352; emphasis added).

The positive aspect of this double-sided coin is the "thy will" approach to working with our Heavenly Father. This consecrated attitude is similar to the "my will" attitude only in that adversity, trials, or tragedies may also be seen as a wall looming in the path ahead. The difference for a "thy will" person is that the wall is not perceived as being insurmountable. The view of the "thy will" person is proactive or solution-driven, as opposed to the reactive nature of the "my will" person. Another difference is in the individual's willingness to face, and even endure, this obstacle with the help of the Lord. Any event of opposition or tragedy is dealt with by approaching Heavenly Father for strength and understanding and always seeking to recognize his will in the process. This view accepts that God's role is that of a trusted Father in Heaven who will allow us to be tried in our best interest, with the promise that we will not be tested beyond that which we are able to bear (1 Corinthians 10:23).

A "thy will" view of life's challenges and tragedies assumes that growth often comes in the midst of the struggle and that inner peace in mortality is obtained through commitment and consecration. However, this perspective does not rob the individual of initiative or agency. The fundamental difference in this attitude, as compared to a "my will" perspective, is the willingness to work with Heavenly Father and trust in him. The "thy will" view sees life as being more than just life here in mortality. While the Lord may see fit to make an obstacle in life's path just go away, that is the Lord's option rather than the constant expectation on the part of the individual.

Incorporated in this concept is the doctrine of enduring to the end, which assumes the notion of being "willing to submit to all things which the Lord seeth fit to inflict upon him, even as a child doth submit to his father" (Mosiah 3:19).

Elder Robert D. Hales spoke of using a "thy will" approach during our prayers: "Gratitude is a divine principle: 'Thou shalt thank the Lord thy God in all things' (D&C 59:7). This scripture means that we should express thankfulness for what happens, not only for the good things in life but also for the opposition and challenges of life that add to our experience and faith. We put our lives in His hands, realizing that all that transpires will be for our experience. When we say in prayer, *'Thy will be done,'* we are really expressing faith and gratitude and acknowledging that we will accept whatever happens in our lives" ("Gratitude for the Goodness of God," *Ensign,* May 1992, 65; emphasis added).

Elder Graham W. Doxey spoke of the peace that can come to us from the Lord when we are truly consecrated: "We must learn to pray with meaning, 'Not my will, but Thy will be done.' When you are able to do this, his whisperings to you will be loud and clear. The Prophet Joseph Smith, after five months of extreme suffering in the dungeon of Liberty Jail, experienced it, and he said, 'When the heart is *sufficiently contrite,* then the voice of inspiration steals along and whispers, My son, peace be unto thy soul'" ("The Voice Is Still Small,"

Ensign, November 1991, 26).

President James E. Faust referred to the practical application of a "thy will" attitude: "Recently I met with a family who had lost a precious son through an unfortunate automobile accident. They wondered when the comforting spirit of the Holy Ghost would envelop them to sustain them. My counsel was that when they were prepared to say to the Lord, 'Thy will be done,' then would come the sweet peace which the Savior promised. This willing submission to the Father is what the Savior exemplified in the Garden of Gethsemane" ("The Grand Key-Words for the Relief Society," *Ensign,* November 1996, 96).

Many moments in our life with Boyd were covered with a dark cloud. It would be untrue to say that we dealt with each challenge with a consistent "thy will" perspective. I will say, however, that during Boyd's ordeal, when we were able to maintain a "thy will" perspective, we were often blessed by a feeling of peace that gave us a strength beyond our own capacities. Conversely, we noticed a difference during those times when our attitude reflected a "my will" perspective.

Obtaining strength beyond our own capacities was defined long ago by the Lord to the Nephite faithful: "I will also ease the burdens which are put upon your shoulders, that even you cannot feel them upon your backs" (Mosiah 24:14).

There are a number of ways of easing burdens. The first is to remove them quickly; another way is to ease them over a period of time. A third way is to strengthen the back that bears the burden placed upon it. Obviously, in this third way of easing burdens, a change must take place within the individual carrying the heavy load. This gives the person a capacity to lift and endure the burden in a blessed "thy will" partnership with the Lord. Mormon describes this event by saying, "The Lord did *strengthen them* that they could bear up their burdens with ease, and they did submit cheerfully and with patience" (Mosiah 24:15; emphasis added).

We can see this same effect in the life of the Prophet Joseph Smith. From Liberty Jail, in a time of anguish and deep suffering for the gospel's sake, he wrote the following message to the Saints: "Dear brethren, do not think that our hearts faint, as though some strange thing had happened unto us, for we have seen and been assured of all these things beforehand, and have assurance of a better hope than that of our persecutors. *Therefore God hath made broad our shoulders for the burden.* We glory in our tribulation, because we know that God is with us, that He is our friend" (*Teachings of the Prophet Joseph Smith,* sel. Joseph Fielding Smith [Salt Lake City: Deseret Book, 1976], 123).

President Thomas S. Monson spoke of this concept of broadening our shoulders to carry life's burdens, saying, "When we are on the Lord's errand, we are entitled to the Lord's help. Remember that *the Lord will shape the back to bear the burden placed upon it*" ("To Learn, to Do, to Be," *Ensign,* May 1992, 48; emphasis added).

This broadening of the back by the Lord is the reason death becomes sweet for those who die unto the Lord (D&C 42:46). It is easy to understand that dying was sweet for Boyd because death was a part of the path that led him back to his Heavenly Father. But how could it have been sweet for those of us who were left behind? The sweetness came from the fact that our shoulders were broadened and strengthened by the Lord for the burden placed upon them. We received a peace and a calm that not only empowered us but also acted like a spiritual anesthesia against the pain of the moment. I know that this blessing came to my wife and me for a short season, both during and after the passing of our son.

It is as if those of us here in mortality are in a weight room filled with all of the equipment used to strengthen and build physical and spiritual muscle. Someone who wants to be strong and grow must be willing to submit to the work required for growth. The person who has worked hard consistently is able to see himself progress and build. When he approaches the weights, he carries with him a completely different attitude from that of the weekend warrior who occasionally enters this workout arena.

A person with a "my will" perspective stands before the long, steel bar of adversity with its heavy weights fastened on both ends. Unprepared to bear the load, he asks God to remove the weight from the bar so that he can lift it. He can raise the bar above the ground only by taking the weights off, and therefore his growth is minimal. The Lord stands willing and able to do so much more for this person but holds back because of the person's lack of preparation.

In contrast, imagine a "thy will" group that has consistently attended the spiritual weight room. They have been working with the instructor—Heavenly Father—so that when the overwhelming weight of adversity is placed before them, they can rely on him to strengthen their backs to lift the bar. They are able to lift the bar, not because the weight has been removed but because a change has taken place in them. The muscles in their backs were strengthened through their faith in God and their desire to do whatever he asked of them—even to the extent that they are able to "submit cheerfully and with patience" (Mosiah 24:15). This strengthening, or broadening, of the back is a spiritual gift that exceeds any strength a person can acquire by trusting solely in the arm of flesh.

The only people I have seen in a typical weight room who are cheerful and patient are those who have been built up physically to the point that their muscles have been strengthened, even under the burden of some very heavy weights. This is just as true in spiritual weight rooms, where the weights of adversity, pain, affliction, and opposition become a great testing ground here in mortality. The Lord may choose to remove the weight, even for people with a "thy will" perspective. The point is that they understand that this is his decision rather than theirs. The "thy will" perspective is being willing to do whatever is necessary to accomplish the will of the Lord.

Developing a "thy will" perspective is one of the major things we have to learn in order to carry on in faith. In our weakest moments, each of us may blame God or lose faith in his influence in our lives. At these times, we are all at a "my will, thy will" crossroads. How we deal with those feelings can set a spiritual course for our lives that allows us to work hand in hand with our Heavenly Father or places us at a distance from his assistance. The test, then, lies in our willingness to pay the consistent price necessary to lift the weight of life's adversities.

Reflect on these words by President Benson: "There are times when you simply have to righteously hang on and outlast the devil until his depressive spirit leaves you. . . . To press on in noble endeavors, even while surrounded by a cloud of depression, will eventually bring you out on top into the sunshine" ("Do Not Despair," *Ensign,* November 1974, 67).

Throughout the many hours that we spent with Boyd in the hospital, we experienced a number of events that had an impact on our lives. One of these was not directly connected to Boyd but helped me to understand the "thy will" perspective we needed in order to deal with cystic fibrosis.

During the long and difficult hours we spent at our son's hospital bedside, I often tried to be productive by reading, writing, or doing just about anything I could think of to pass the time valuably. Even doing this, I would sometimes get tired of sitting. On many of those occasions at the hospital, I would go for a walk to clear my head. Located near the cystic fibrosis clinic was the burn unit and rehabilitation area.

I often witnessed pain that gave me an appreciation for the much greater suffering of our Lord in Gethsemane. I saw doctors and nurses bring in people who were burned so badly that I could not immediately discern if they were lying face up or face down. At first glance, I couldn't tell if they were male or female, black or white, or where their clothes stopped and their skin began. They would often "air vac" these poor souls in by helicopter and hurry them down a hallway to a room that was used for washing the wounds and removing the victim's burned skin. In fact, unless these people were placed in a vat of liquid that removed and cleansed their skin, many of them would not have survived.

As hospital personnel worked with these victims, at times their screams of pain seemed to be coming from animals rather than humans. In between these vocal shrieks of agony, some patients would verbally strike out against nurses and doctors, even to the point of making physical threats at them. In their agony, they misunderstood the role of the person before them, who appeared to be the cause of their pain.

The patience and empathy of these good people toward the burn victims was admirable. I'm sure there were exceptions, but I never saw them interpret the verbal abuse directed toward them as being personal. Experience had taught them that even though the patient could die without going through the process, it was only natural for the burn victim to resist anything that brought such tremendous pain.

In many ways, the prolonged, agonizing process of recovery is more painful for the burn victim than the actual event of being burned. I have witnessed a few of these burn victims give up on themselves, but as long as there was a chance at recovery, I never witnessed a burn unit worker give up on a patient.

We can easily liken the roles of patient and therapist to our relationship with our Heavenly Father. In our own situation with Boyd—with all the pain and suffering—our greatest error would have been to view our Heavenly Father as the problem rather than the solution. God's arm is "lengthened out" continually on our behalf (2 Nephi 28:32). The question is how we deal with his outstretched arm. Just as with the burn victims, there will be pain associated with growth and recovery. Having a "my will" attitude and not being willing to submit and endure is to handicap the therapist's ability to assist. This is as true of God as it is in a hospital burn unit. The patient who feels the therapist is not his friend places himself at a distance from his greatest advocate.

The most severe burn victims have to go through a long, drawn-out process that often takes years. Even if a burn victim has suffered burns on most of his body, skin grafts still must come from that victim's own body. After a portion of unburned skin is taken from one part of the body and grafted into another part of the body, the patient has to wait a long period of time for the skin to grow back enough to be grafted again.

During this time, the patient spends a great deal of time in bed. This inactivity causes muscles and joints to atrophy. Therefore, on a regular basis a therapist must work with the patient to strengthen him and help him with range of motion. A burned arm or leg needs to be able to extend to its maximum range of mobility before a skin graft can be performed.

Before making a skin graft, a therapist regularly assists the patient in the painful, often excruciating, process of exercising the joints to attain this maximum mobility. To do this, the therapist has to push the patient's arm or leg beyond what the atrophied limb, as well as the overworked burn victim, is able to do. Periodically, the verbal rebellion of the patient that often accompanies this exercise is directed at the therapist.

With few exceptions, the therapists I saw seemed to exercise the compassion and charity that was necessary. As time passed and the patients began to see their progression toward recovery, it seemed to me that many of these burn victims viewed their therapist as a type of savior.

Over time, as a natural result of their recovery, they were able to leave the hospital. On their return visits, it was obvious from the way they treated the professionals at whom they had once directed their deepest anger that more than just their burns had healed. They had gained a fuller appreciation for those who would not give up on them in their darkest hour.

There were elements of our experience with our son that I could easily connect to the emotions of the burn victims, who struggled to gain a working relationship with their therapist. I have a feeling that when we meet our divine therapist on the other side of the veil and see mortality with full clarity, we will thank the Lord for many of the things that brought us the most pain here in this life. We will thank him for those things that brought us to our knees and, eventually, to him. As I ponder the trials connected to Boyd's life and death, it is only in looking at this bigger picture that peace comes to my soul.

I hope that through sharing our experience, others will be encouraged to press forward, endure, change a "my will" attitude, or do whatever is appropriate to fully appreciate life, including its challenges. Our family has felt the influence of the Spirit in our lives most consistently when we have maintained the proper perspective. In our best moments, we have had a glimpse of what life could be if we were able to maintain this view continually.

The answers for the specific needs of others may not be met by likening our experience to theirs. I am convinced, however, that in developing a "thy will" perspective—by placing total trust in the Lord—the answers, as well as the desired peace of mind, will come.

EPILOGUE

One of the qualities I have discovered in people with a healthy outlook on life is that they do not define themselves by the negative things that may be happening around, or even to, them. They understand that stormy weather is a fact of life that each of us must deal with.

During a difficult rainstorm, if we believed that harsh conditions were here to stay, our attitude would naturally be consumed by the weather. Those of us with a healthy attitude are able to deal with all kinds of circumstances because we accept the truth that bad weather is temporary, or seasonal, and certainly not here to stay. When we define ourselves by the storms in our lives, we fail to enjoy the sunlight in our misguided efforts to shield ourselves from the next cloudburst (Neal A. Maxwell, *One More Strain of Praise* [Salt Lake City: Bookcraft, 1999], 29).

Even after all these years, there are days when thoughts

of my son's passing are hard to deal with. However, these harsh-weather moments have been more clearly defined for me with the passing of time. Understanding that our lives, as well as the lives of those we love, continue beyond mortality has allowed me to accept Boyd's absence as a part of the weather I must pass through. It has been the healing rays of the Son that have allowed me to carry on in the hope of a joyful reunion. On those days when discouragement seems to dictate the climate around me, it has been this hope that has allowed me to work my way through the clouds of despair and travel toward a brighter outlook.

At the beginning of this book, I shared the experience I had of being a spectator to my barber's singing. Little did I know that there would be times following my son's death that if my thoughts and feelings had been expressed as music, then surely they would have come forth from the depths of my soul as the blues. Time has taught me that this feeling is not uncommon for people. I believe that how we respond to these blues has a way of defining us.

Influenced by the bad weather? Yes. Defined by the storms? Never! Those who choose to live by the lyrics of the song appropriately titled "Stormy Weather" have played this broken record for so long that they seem forever destined to sing the Blues. Even during my most difficult moments, I had the feeling that somehow my heart would one day heal and that I would be able to sing songs of joy once more. I believe this was a gift from the Savior.

I have come to understand that the power of the songs sung by my barber friend was not found in the quality of his singing but in the fact that he still believed in the beauty and value of life, even in the midst of pain. He had made the decision that every productive person must make—to look for the "Son-shine," even in the midst of life's storms. The words of this book are my effort to do the same. These words, then, become the lyrics of my song. The ability to sing is not a gift the Lord has given me. Because of my inabilities, the actual melody will have to go unheard. But in the absence of music, I hope that the reader will be strengthened by my singing praises to Christ and his atoning sacrifice in the words of this book. Because of him, I know that I will be with my son again. In witness of this truth, I add my voice to the choirs of people who have sung before.

APPENDIX

Did Christ take upon himself more than sin in Gethsemane?
(from chapter 1)

The following words of the Brethren have been a great comfort to my wife and me as we have tried to understand the path that lay ahead of us:

Elder Neal A. Maxwell alluded to my question when he said, "The Savior knows what it's like to die from cancer" (*Even As I Am* [Salt Lake City: Deseret Book, 1982], 116–17). The Savior obviously did not die of cancer on the cross, but his encounter with other "infirmities" was part of the Gethsemane experience.

On another occasion, Elder Maxwell stated: "He showed condescension when he chose to suffer, not only for our sins, but for the infirmities, sicknesses, and illnesses of mankind. But the agonies of the Atonement were infinite and first-hand! Since not all human sorrow and pain is connected to sin, the full intensiveness of the Atonement involved bearing our pains, infirmities, and sicknesses, as well as our sin" (in *Doctrines of the Book of Mormon: 1991 Sperry Symposium on the Book of Mormon* [Salt Lake City: Deseret Book, 1992], 87).

This same apostle stated in general conference, "He [Christ] felt our pains and afflictions before we did and knows how to succor us" ("'Swallowed Up in the Will of the Father,'" *Ensign,* November 1995, 24).

When we consider the magnitude of the Savior's atoning sacrifice and all of the elements involved in Gethsemane, it may be hard to contemplate this event on a personal level beyond that of Christ's involvement. Elder Merrill J. Bateman stated, "Whatever the source of pain, Jesus . . . knows each of us personally. . . . In the garden and on the cross, Jesus saw each of us and . . . experienced our deepest feelings so that he would know how to comfort and strengthen us" ("The Power to Heal from Within," *Ensign,* May 1995, 14).

What a great comfort it is to realize that our Savior took more than sin—including the suffering of cystic fibrosis—upon himself and that Christ saw each of us, including my son Boyd. To know about Christ is important, but to know Christ personally, in the sense of what he has done for us in Gethsemane, requires more that just a general understanding—it requires experience.

Personal desires and priesthood blessings
(from chapter 1)

As I searched for an explanation for why I was not prompted by the Spirit to give the blessing I desired to give, I read these words of Brigham Young: "How often have we sealed blessings of health and life upon our children and companions in the name of Jesus Christ and by the authority of the Holy Priesthood . . . and yet our faith and prayers did not succeed in accomplishing the desires of our hearts. Why is this? In many instances our anxiety is so great that we do not pause to know the spirit of revelation. . . . We have anxiety instead of faith. He lays his hands upon the sick, but they are not healed. It is in consequence of not being completely molded to the Will of God" (in *Journal of Discourses,* 26 vols.

[London: Latter-day Saints' Book Depot, 1854–86], 12:125).

Elder Dallin H. Oaks stated in general conference: "Faith, no matter how strong it is, cannot produce a result contrary to the will of him whose power it is. The exercise of faith in the Lord Jesus Christ is always subject to the order of heaven, to the goodness and will and wisdom and timing of the Lord. That is why we cannot have true faith in the Lord without also having complete trust in the Lord's will and in the Lord's timing" ("Faith in the Lord Jesus Christ," *Ensign,* May 1994, 100).

Even in exercising all the faith we have, we must realize that the will of the Lord must dictate the outcome of our priesthood blessings. J. Reuben Clark Jr., a former member of the First Presidency, said: "I do not believe that the Lord . . . permits any man to have faith that would overrule his purposes. In that connection, I call to your attention the fact that the Savior himself pled that his crucifixion might be turned aside. Yet, on one occasion he said, when he asked that the hour might be passed on, '. . . but for this cause came I unto this hour' (John 12:27). The Son of God was not given the necessary faith at the time to enable him to turn aside the purposes reached by himself and the Father before" (in Roy W. Doxey, *The Latter-day Prophets and the Doctrine and Covenants* [Salt Lake City: Deseret Book, 1978], 91).

This next passage is thought to have come from the pen of Samuel O. Bennion: "While it is true that God has conferred upon mortal man the priesthood by which, within certain limitations, they have power to act in his name, it is not true that he has conferred upon them the keys of life and death. . . . By the prayer of faith they can often influence the result, but the decision always rests with God" (*Liahona, the Elders'*

Journal 6 [June 5, 1909]: 1227–28).

President Spencer W. Kimball wrote: "I am grateful that even through the Priesthood I cannot heal all the sick. I might heal people who should die, I might relieve people of suffering who should suffer. I fear I would frustrate the purposes of God. Would you dare to take the responsibility of bringing back to life your loved one? I, myself, would hesitate to do so. I am grateful that we may always pray: 'Thy will be done in all things, for Thou knowest what is best.' I am glad I do not have the decisions to make" (*Faith Precedes the Miracle* [Salt Lake City: Bookcraft, 1972], 7–8).

An experience I had while serving as a full-time missionary many years ago in Brighton, England, illustrates the need to respond to the whisperings of the Spirit while giving priesthood blessings rather than projecting our own will.

A nonmember sister from Australia suffered a heart attack while she was on holiday in southern England. While lying in her hospital bed, she recalled an experience she had when two elders in Australia gave a blessing of healing to someone close to her. It had made such an impression on her that at this point in her life, she hoped she might find missionaries who could give her a blessing. She asked one of the nurses to look up the LDS missionaries in the phone book and extend her desire to receive a blessing.

Even though I had been in the mission field for a few months, this was the first time I had been asked to give a blessing. To complicate matters a bit, my senior companion and I were not working together on that particular evening. My companion was a young Englishman who had been ordained to the Melchizedek Priesthood the previous Sunday. In other words, neither one of us had ever given a blessing before.

As we entered the hospital, my heart was full of anxiety. I wanted to share my fears with my companion, but I was afraid of what it might do to his faith because I was the senior elder for the evening.

I had a testimony of the truthfulness of the gospel, but now I was being asked to do something that required a greater kind of faith. I had never been asked to draw on the powers of heaven in this way before. It was a lot easier to believe the Church was true than it was to represent the Lord in this fashion. My mind was racing with self-doubt, along with just trying to remember the correct words I was to use to begin the blessing. What was I going to say when I placed my hands on that poor lady's head? Did I have enough faith to be in tune with the Lord?

My thoughts were interrupted as we entered her hospital room. I was a bit taken aback by her appearance. The numerous wires and tubes connected to her gave the impression that she was not doing well at all. To make matters more challenging, she was not conscious. I couldn't tell whether she was sleeping or sedated, and I didn't want to wake her up to find out.

As I approached her bed to proceed with the blessing, my fears were at their highest point. My companion interrupted my anxiety by stating, "I have never given a priesthood blessing before. With your permission, I would be honored to offer the blessing if you would do the anointing." I tried to appear gracious in acceding to his request. Actually, I was relieved beyond measure.

Following the anointing, we reverently placed our hands on her head, and he began to speak. He didn't waste many words as he commanded her to be healed. It seemed somehow strange that as we administered to her she was not consciously aware of what was happening. I asked him on the way out of the hospital if he realized what he had told her in the blessing.

His reply was almost as short as the blessing: "I think I spoke as the Spirit directed."

Later in the evening, I got back together with my regular companion, and I told him about the blessing. He stated that if she was interested enough to receive a priesthood blessing, then we had better follow up with her to see if she might wish to be taught the discussions.

The next day we went to the hospital to visit her. As we entered her room, we noticed that not only was her bed vacant but also that the portable dresser next to it had been cleaned out. My first thought was, "Oh my, she must have died during the night."

Just then a nurse, who recognized me from the night before, entered the room. We inquired after the whereabouts of our friend, to which she replied, "The strangest thing happened last night after you left. She awoke and said she felt great. We ran tests on her this morning that indicated she was doing fine. She asked to be released this afternoon. For all we know, she's on her way back to Australia."

As I pondered this experience, I understood to a greater degree that even though I felt dwarfed by the responsibility of calling down the powers of heaven, the Lord was still able to exercise his power. I pondered the possibility that the woman never even knew she had received a blessing; certainly, she had not been aware of the powerful words of the newly ordained elder. I also realized that it was the Lord who had healed her; my companion had just responded to the Lord's will.

Over the years I have learned to be open to the promptings of the Spirit and to try to say only those things that the Lord inspires me to say while giving a blessing. I have learned never to place my desires in the blessing, hoping that it might somehow force the Lord to conform to my wishes. The authority of the priesthood gives us the opportunity to respond to the Lord's will and nothing beyond that.

The first line of defense
(from chapter 3)

I have discovered that on those occasions when I hastily digest the hurtful words of others without making the effort to look for the best in the person who delivered them, I am sometimes left with the false conclusion that I am a child of God while the person who has injured me is not. The logical extension of this improper thinking is that I feel no obligation to practice Christian injunctions, which would prevent me from judging or even hating this person who has wrongfully injured me. When I allow myself to travel this mental path, it becomes impossible for me to exercise any kind of charitable compassion toward others, and often times my only emotional response is to judge or verbally attack the person who has threatened me. Thus, I become more connected to the problem than to the solution; I have justified my own misbehavior by thinking, "He did it to me first."

It is difficult to see clearly when our first reaction in a conflict is to place blame. Placing blame or attacking verbally takes no skill because these are the reactions of the "natural man" (Mosiah 3:19). The ultimate result of this kind of thinking, when spread throughout the world, is that the commandment "thou shalt not kill" is true, except for bad guys because they are not children of God like us. It is hard for some people to see that the physical violence in our world today is inseparably connected to the passive violence we have toward others in our attitudes as well as in our conversations.

Arun Gandhi, grandson of Mahatma Gandhi, spoke on this subject to the students of Brigham Young University:

> We are often so focused on the physical violence that we don't look at the passive violence we do against people. . . . Passive can be either conscious or unconscious. We don't use any physical force, but our body language, our attitudes, the way we speak to people, the way we look at people, the things that we do and say to people—all of these can be acts of violence. Actually, it is the passive violence we commit all the time—knowingly or unknowing—that generates anger in the victim, and that anger then translates into physical violence. In effect, passive violence fuels the fire of physical violence.
>
> If we want to put out the fire of physical violence, logically we have to cut off the fuel supply. And the fuel supply is us. . . . I'm sure if I ask all of you now whether you are violent or nonviolent, you will all be willing to swear on the Bible that you are nonviolent. But we are nonviolent only in the sense that we don't go out and beat up people or kill people. But we are violent in the sense that we practice a lot of passive violence, and unless we acknowledge and change that, we'll never be able to create a peaceful society. . . .
>
> One Saturday my father had to go to town to attend a conference, and he didn't feel like driving, so he asked me if I would drive him into town and bring him back in the evening. . . . Since I was going into town, my mom gave me a list of groceries she needed, and on the way into town, my dad told me that there were many small chores

that had been pending for a long time, like getting the car serviced and the oil changed.

When I left my father at the conference venue, he said, 'At 5 o'clock in the evening, I will wait for you outside this auditorium. Come here and pick me up, and we'll go home together.'

I said, 'Fine.' I rushed off and I did all my chores as quickly as possible—I bought the groceries, I left the car in the garage with instructions to do whatever was necessary—and I went straight to the nearest movie theater. In those days, being a 16-year-old, I was extremely interested in cowboy movies. . . . I got so engrossed in a John Wayne double feature that I didn't realize the passage of time. The movie ended at 5:30, and I came out and ran to the garage and rushed to where Dad was waiting for me. It was almost 6 o'clock when I reached there, and he was anxious and pacing up and down wondering what had happened to me. The first question he asked me was, 'Why are you late?'

Instead of telling him the truth, I lied to him, and I said, 'The car wasn't ready; I had to wait for the car,' not realizing that he had already called the garage.

When he caught me in the lie, he said, 'There's something wrong in the way I brought you up that didn't give you the confidence to tell me the truth, that made you feel you had to lie to me. I've got to find out where I went wrong with you, and to do that,' he said, 'I'm going to walk home—18 miles. I'm not coming with you in the car.' There was absolutely nothing I could do to make him change his mind.

It was after 6 o'clock in the evening when he started walking. Much of those 18 miles were through sugar-cane plantations—dirt roads, no lights, it was late in the night—and I couldn't leave him and go away. For five and a half hours I crawled along in the car behind Father, watching him go through all this pain and agony for a stupid lie. I decided there and then that I was never going to lie again. . . .

Now, that is the power of nonviolent action. It's a lasting thing. It's a change we bring through love, not a change we bring through fear. Anything that is brought by fear doesn't last. But anything that is done by love lasts forever" ("Reflections of Peace," *Brigham Young Magazine,* Spring 2000, 37–43)

Accepting ourselves, judging others
(from chapter 3)

The following is a story by my niece Janae Howells, who, at the age of thirteen, was diagnosed as having aplastic anemia, an illness that causes the bone marrow to cease manufacturing blood cells.

When I arrived at UCLA Medical Center for the bone marrow transplant, it seemed like a bad dream from which I couldn't wake up. It was hard to imagine that it was really happening to me. After the transplant, when the chemotherapy and radiation started to affect my hair, I lost it within a day and a half. I decided not to look at myself in the mirror. I would avoid seeing myself as long as possible.

But then I saw my reflection in the faucet. It scared me! I couldn't believe it was me. Then I realized how sick I really was. It hit me and I realized that it wasn't a dream and I had to deal with reality.

I sat down with my mom and cried and talked out my feelings. I decided that no matter what people said or did to me, I was me and nobody could change that. Mom and I learned, "It's not what happens to you but the way you handle it that counts." I had many opportunities to learn how to develop this belief.

My first encounter was when I was able to go outdoors when my hair was about one inch long, yet I couldn't be in a confined area with people except my own family. I rode my bike with my sister, Rebecca, to the 7–Eleven store. I was waiting outside for her when a couple of boys walked past and said, "Hey, kid, cute sandals!" In other words, they thought I was a boy wearing sissy shoes. Even though I knew this was going to be one of many experiences, it still didn't make it easy.

Finally, I was able to go to the mall as long as I wore a mask. I decided to wear a hat too. It was actually a hand-made turban from my grandmother to cover my nearly bald head. Because of that, people gave me compassionate looks and I felt comfortable.

Then my big day came! The doctor said I would be able to go to Beehive Camp and be with people my own age and be without a mask. My hair was about two inches long. I was excited because it was the longest it had been in six months. Because that was such an improvement for me, I had not realized that it was still quite short to others. There were many at Beehive Camp that didn't know me or of my experience. I would hear people say, "Oh, look at her, I wonder why she cut her hair so short' or 'I wonder who she is."

After hearing these comments, I would walk off by myself and cry or go into the cabin and lie down and hide my face. Then I would remember, "It's not what happens to me; it's the way I handle it." Then I would decide to go out and face reality.

At school I was called "weirdo" and "stupid." It wasn't just children and teenagers who gave me a hard time, it was also adults. One such time was when I was able to go to the mall without my mask and hat. By now my hair was just over two inches long. As I walked by, a few adults . . . [gave] me repulsive looks and let me know how disgusted they were at the younger generation.

I struggled with feelings of "Well, they don't know my situation. They don't even know me!" I'd think to myself, "If this shocks them, I should dye my hair purple and then see what they do." Changing my hair color was just a passing thought, but I tried different responses such as giving them dirty looks in return. But changing my facial expressions didn't work because they would just walk off—convinced that their belief of me was correct. Next, I would smile and try to send a caring, loving look. However, this backfired because they would be surprised and walk off embarrassed.

I feel that I have learned a great lesson from this experience: That it is not my place to judge others, no matter how they look. My responsibility is to accept and love them no matter how they treat me.

The great lesson in this story for Boyd and all of us is that it's not so much what happens to you but the way you handle it that counts. By responding improperly to society's negative input, we truly handicap ourselves. Our attitude makes all the difference.

The spirit world all around us
(from chapter 4)

While experiences involving visitors from the spirit world may seem unusual to many people in this day and age, members of The Church of Jesus Christ of Latter-day Saints are not surprised at the possibility of such events. The Prophet Joseph Smith said, "The spirits of the just are not far from us, and know and understand our thoughts, feelings, and motions" (*Teachings of the Prophet Joseph Smith,* sel. Joseph Fielding Smith [Salt Lake City: Deseret Book, 1976], 326).

On one occasion, Elder George Q. Cannon stated, "If our eyes were open to see the spirit world around us, . . . we would not be so unguarded and careless and so indifferent; . . . we would be continually watchful and prayerful to our Heavenly Father for His Holy Spirit and *His holy angels* to be around about us to strengthen us" *(Gospel Truth: Discourses and Writings of George Q. Cannon,* sel. Jerreld L. Newquist, 2 vols. in 1 [Salt Lake City: Deseret Book, 1974], 1:82; emphasis added).

President Brigham Young said, "Where is the spirit world? . . . Can you see spirits in this room? No. Suppose the Lord should touch your eyes that you might see, could you then see the spirits? Yes, as plainly as you now see bodies" (*Discourses of Brigham Young,* sel. John A. Widtsoe [Salt Lake City: Deseret Book, 1954], 377).

In our own time Elder Vaughn J. Featherstone said: "There is no safety in the world. . . . As the evil night darkens upon this generation, we must come to the temple for light and safety. . . . Unseen sentinels oftentimes watch over us. . . . Surely angelic attendants guard the temples of the Most High. . . . There will be greater hosts of *unseen beings* in the temples. Prophets of old as well as those in this dispensation will visit the temples. Those who attend will feel their strength and feel their companionship. We will not be alone in our temples" (Vaughn J. Featherstone, CES memorandum, November 21, 1994).

Elder Heber C. Kimball recorded many experiences involving angels. Speaking of Zion's Camp, he wrote, "We did not fear, nor hesitate to proceed on our journey, for God was with us, and angels went before us, and we had no fear of either men or devils. This we knew because they (the angels) were seen" (Orson F. Whitney, *Life of Heber C. Kimball: An Apostle, the Father and Founder of the British Mission* [Salt Lake City: Stevens & Wallis, 1945], 43–44).

He also bore his testimony regarding the daily administration of angels: "I know that God lives and dwells in the heavens. . . . He is not so far off as many imagine. He is near by, His angels are our associates, they are with us and around about us, and watch over us, and take care of us, and lead us, and guide us, and administer to our wants in their ministry and in their holy calling unto which they are appointed. We are told in the Bible that angels are ministering spirits to minister to those who shall become heirs of salvation. We have the spirits of the ancients, also, administering to the Saints: Who have you now in your midst? Have you Abraham and Isaac and the Apostles Peter, James and John? Yes, you have them right in your midst—they are talking to you all the time" (Whitney, *Life of Heber C. Kimball,* 460–61).

The Prophet Joseph Smith said this about the dedication of the Kirtland Temple: "A noise was heard like the sound of a rushing mighty wind, which filled the Temple. . . . I beheld the Temple was filled with angels, which fact I declared to the congregation" (*History of The Church of Jesus Christ of Latter-day Saints,* ed. B. H. Roberts, 2d ed. rev., 7 vols. [Salt Lake City: The Church of Jesus Christ of Latter-day Saints, 1932–51], 2:427–28).

During a missionary meeting in Scotland, a young Elder David O. McKay witnessed the administration of angels: "During the progress of the meeting, an elder on his own initiative arose and said, 'Brethren, there are angels in this room.' . . . President James L. McMurrin arose and confirmed that statement by pointing to one brother sitting just in front of me and saying, 'Yes, brethren, there are angels in this room, and one of them is the guardian angel of that young man sitting there,' and he designated one who today is a patriarch of the Church. Pointing to another elder, he said, 'And one is the guardian angel of that young man there,' and he singled out one whom I had known from childhood" (David O. McKay, *Cherished Experiences,* comp. Clare Middlemus [Salt Lake City: Deseret Book, 1955], 12–14).

President Harold B. Lee bore his witness in the April 1973 general conference: "I was suffering from an ulcer condition that was becoming worse and worse. We had been touring a mission; my wife, Joan, and I were impressed the next morning that we should get home as quickly as possible. . . . On the way across the country, we were sitting in the forward section of the airplane. . . . As we approached a certain point en route, someone laid his hand upon my head. I looked up; I could see no one. That happened again before we arrived home, again with the same experience. . . . I knew that I was receiving a blessing [from someone unseen] that I came a few hours later to know I needed most desperately. . . . But, shortly thereafter, there came massive hemorrhages which, had they occurred while we were in flight, I wouldn't be here today talking about it. I know that there are powers divine that reach out when all other help is not available" (*Stand Ye in Holy Places* [Salt Lake City: Deseret Book, 1976], 187–88).

The suffering of the Martin Handcart Company has been well documented. One of the members of the company spoke of the experience many years later: "We suffered beyond anything you can imagine and many died of exposure and starvation. . . . Everyone of us came through with the absolute knowledge that God lives, for we became acquainted with him in our extremities. I have pulled my handcart when I was so weak and weary from illness and lack of food that I could hardly put one foot ahead of the other. I have looked ahead and seen a patch of sand or a hill slope and I have said, I can go only that far and there I must give up, for I cannot pull the load through it. . . . I have gone on to that sand and when I reached it, the cart began pushing me. I have looked back many times to see who was pushing my cart, but my eyes saw no one. I knew then that *the angels of God were there*. . . . The price we paid to become acquainted with God was a privilege to pay, and I am thankful that I was privileged to come in the Martin Handcart Company" (David O. McKay, "Pioneer Women," *Relief Society Magazine,* January 1948, 8; emphasis added).

Our circumstances are known to God
(from chapter 4)

Regarding the birth of children, President Spencer W. Kimball said: "God does nothing by chance, but always by design as a loving father. *The manner of our coming into the world, our parents, the time, and other circumstances of our birth and condition, are all according to eternal purposes, direction, and appointment of divine Providence*" ("Small Acts of Service," *Ensign,* December 1974, 5; emphasis added).

This same prophet wrote: "I believe we may die prematurely but seldom exceed our time very much. . . . I am positive in my mind that the Lord has planned our destiny. Sometime we'll understand fully, and when we see back from the vantage point of the future, we shall be satisfied with many of the happenings of this life that are so difficult for us to comprehend. . . . We eagerly accepted the chance to come earthward even though it might be for only a day or a year" (*Faith Precedes the Miracle* [Salt Lake City: Deseret Book, 1972], 104–6).

President Henry D. Moyle, a former member of the First Presidency, said these words in general conference: "We had our own free agency in our pre-mortal existence, and whatever we are today is likely the result of that which we willed to be heretofore. *We unquestionably knew before we elected to come to this earth the conditions under which we would here exist.* . . . We are exactly what we should be, each one of us, except as we may have altered that pattern by deviating from the laws of God here in mortality" (in Conference Reports of The Church of Jesus Christ of Latter-day Saints [Salt Lake City: The Church of Jesus Christ of Latter-day Saints, 1898 to present], October 1952, 71–72).

After stating that Christ knew of his trials before he accepted his mortal body, Joseph F. Smith wrote regarding us, "*If Christ knew beforehand, so did we.* But in coming here, we forgot all, that our agency might be free indeed, to choose good or evil" (*Gospel Doctrine* [Salt Lake City: Deseret Book, 1975], 13; emphasis added).

Elder Bruce R. McConkie wrote, "Our Eternal Father knows all of his spirit children, and in his infinite wisdom, he chooses the very time that each comes to earth to gain a mortal body. . . . And each of these children is subjected to the very trials and experiences that Omniscient Wisdom knows he should have" (*The Millennial Messiah: The Second Coming of the Son of Man* [Salt Lake City: Deseret Book, 1982], 660).

The experience of Danish convert Niels P. L. Eskildz indicates that so many of life's events, which appear to be happenstance or even tragedies, may have divine undertones. Niels was seriously crippled and deformed at the age of ten. For sixteen years he suffered pain and great despair. But just before his baptism in 1862, he had a revelation that changed his disposition regarding his own infirmities: "While engaged preparing his evening meal a glorious vision burst upon his view. . . . He comprehended . . . that he had witnessed a somewhat similar scene in his premortal state. . . . He knew that he had deliberately made his choice. He . . . understood that such a reward [for him] was only to be gained by mortal suffering—that, in fact, he must be a cripple and endure severe physical pain, privation and ignominy. He was conscious too that he still insisted upon having that reward, and accepted and agreed to the conditions. He emerged from the vision with a settled conviction, that to rebel against or even to repine at his fate, was not only a reproach to an All-Wise Father whose care had been over him notwithstanding his seeming abandonment, but a base violation of the deliberate promise and agreement he had entered into, and upon the observance of which his future reward depended" (in Duane S. Crowther, *Life Everlasting* [Salt Lake City: Bookcraft, 1967], 39–40).

Can we be tested more than we are able to bear?
(from chapter 5)

Elder Neal A. Maxwell referred to this test when addressing a Brigham Young University audience several years ago: "When in situations of stress we wonder if there is any more in us to give. We can be comforted to know that God, who knows our capacity perfectly, placed us here to succeed. No one was foreordained to fail. . . . Let us remember that we were measured before and were found equal to our tasks. . . . When we feel overwhelmed, let us recall the assurance that God will not over-program us; he will not press upon us more than we can bear" ("A More Determined Discipleship," *Ensign,* February 1979, 69).

Elder Boyd K. Packer stated in general conference: "Some are tested by poor health, some by a body that is deformed or homely. Others are tested by handsome and healthy bodies. . . . All are part of the test. And there is more equality in this testing than sometimes we suspect" ("The Choice," *Ensign,* November 1980, 21).

Even though I despaired at Spencer's health, I was reminded that God is aware of the circumstances in which we enter this world. President Howard W. Hunter echoed the same sentiment when he said, "Each trial in life is tailored to the individual's capacities and needs as known by a loving Father in Heaven" ("'Come unto Me,'" *Ensign,* November 1990, 18).

A parent must deal with each child's sense of self-worth individually (from chapter 5)

The time we spent reinforcing Boyd's worth didn't automatically carry over to our other children. This is a battle that must be won one child at a time. For example, when Spencer was three years old, I found him playing with matches in the backyard. I gave him a royal chewing out in an effort to stop him from ever getting involved in such a dangerous game again.

At the conclusion of my tirade, this little child of God

turned and walked away. As he headed around the corner, I followed him to see if my words had sunk in. Unaware of my watching eyes, he leaned against the side of the house. Speaking to no one in particular, he quietly said, "I don't even like myself."

His words hit me like a knockout punch. He hadn't heard my speech at all! The truth was that I had responded to the pressures that had built up inside me throughout the day, and my method of correcting my son was based as much on those pressures as it was on his playing with matches. Like so many other children, Spencer had responded to the intensity in which the message was delivered rather than the message itself. Actually, the message he digested was that Daddy didn't like him.

Recognizing this, I had to reword my speech so that the level of punishment did not exceed his crime. All too often a child receives the spirit of the message rather than the message itself.

On another occasion many years later, Arlene had an interesting experience with one of our children. As parents, we have discovered that it is sometimes a challenge to teach small children what is and what is not an appropriate restroom. At times, little boys find it easier to answer the call of nature in the out-of-doors rather than taking the time to use the appropriate facilities.

While Arlene and our toddler were out playing in the front yard, without warning, our little son pulled his trousers down and was preparing to urinate on the side of the house. She gently demanded that our son cease such behavior and go into the house to use the bathroom. Quickly searching for a teaching analogy a child could appreciate, she said, "Only dogs stand outside when they go to the restroom."

He willingly pulled up his pants and turned the corner of the house. Assuming he was on his way to the back door, Arlene pursued him in hopes of offering some assistance. To her surprise, he had only changed locations. By the time she reached our son, he had his pants down again.

Surprised at his disobedience, following so soon after her initial counsel, she marched undetected toward him. Her stern posture quickly changed when she heard our toddler chanting, "Arf, arf, arf" in his best canine imitation.

Arlene and I had a good chuckle later that evening when she related the experience to me. Our conversation grew a little more serious as we wondered how our child's actions might have been different if she had said, "Only bad boys go to the restroom on the lawn." We contemplated how a constant barrage of "Only bad boys spill their milk" or "Only bad boys tease their sister" or expressions like "Only bad boys wet their bed" could shape the way a child sees himself over a period of time.

Maybe this is why the Savior warns adults who offend children. It would be better for such people to have a millstone hung about their necks and for them to be drowned in the depths of the sea (Matthew 18:6; Mark 9:42; Luke 17:2; D&C 121:19).

I heard a story a few years ago regarding a famous motivational speaker who was visiting with inmates following a speech he had delivered at a state prison. One of the prisoners asked him to whom he would give the credit for his tremendous success.

After pondering the question for a moment, he said, "I suppose the major credit would have to go to my father. As a boy, he made me feel that I could succeed at anything I tried to do. I guess I heard him say it so many times I started believing it myself."

Another inmate said, "I'm sure your daddy must be proud of you now."

A fellow prisoner lamented his own experience by saying, "My dad told me all through my youth that I was a no-good bum and that I would wind up in prison some day." He continued sarcastically, "I suppose he's really proud of me too."

Quite often our youth rise or fall to the level of confidence their parents genuinely have in them. Because each child develops labels he identifies with, it behooves parents to ensure that those labels are realistically positive and to support children in nurturing a healthy view of themselves.

Concerning death, resurrection, and the fate of little children
(from chapter 7)

President Joseph Fielding Smith said: "A man who has lost a leg in childhood will have his leg restored. . . . . Deformities and the like will be corrected, if not immediately at the time of the uniting of the spirit and body, so soon thereafter [almost instantly] that it will make no difference. . . . Infants and children do not grow in the grave, but when they come forth, they will come forth with the same body and in the same size in which the body was when it was laid away. After the resurrection the body will grow until it has reached the full stature of manhood or womanhood" *(Doctrines of Salvation,* comp. Bruce R. McConkie, 3 vols. [Salt Lake City: Bookcraft, 1954–56], 2:293–94).

President Joseph F. Smith wrote: "When the mother

is deprived of the pleasure and joy of rearing her baby to manhood or to womanhood in this life, through the hand of death, that privilege will be renewed to her hereafter, and she will enjoy it to a fuller fruition than it would be possible for her to do here. When she does it there, it will be with the certain knowledge that the results will be without failure; whereas here, the results are unknown until after we have passed the test" (*Gospel Doctrine* [Salt Lake City: Deseret Book, 1975], 454).

The Prophet Joseph Smith gave these words of comfort to M. Isabella Horne, who had lost a child to death: "The Prophet . . . told us that we should receive those children in the morning of the resurrection just as we laid them down, in purity and innocence, and we should nourish and care for them as their mothers. . . . Children would grow and develop in the Millennium, and . . . mothers would have the pleasure of training and caring for them, which they had been deprived of in this life" (*History of The Church of Jesus Christ of Latter-day Saints,* ed. B. H. Roberts, 2d ed. rev., 7 vols. [Salt Lake City: The Church of Jesus Christ of Latter-day Saints, 1932–51], 4:556–57).

Regarding the ordinances of baptism and temple marriage for children who die before the age of accountability, Joseph Fielding Smith wrote: "All that we need do for children is to have them sealed to their parents. They need no baptism and never will, for our Lord has performed all the work necessary for them. . . . Boys and girls who die after baptism may have the endowment work done for them in the temple. Children who die in infancy do not have to be endowed. So far as the ordinance of sealing [marriage] is concerned, this may wait until the Millennium" (*Doctrines of Salvation,* 2:54–55).

Elder Melvin J. Ballard echoed this sentiment regarding his own son who died at the age of six: "In the Lord's own time my son will have every right to choose a companion and receive the sealing powers that will unite him with one of his own choosing so that he can pass by the gods unto his own exaltation" (*Crusader for Righteousness* [Salt Lake City: Bookcraft, 1966], 278).

Why me?
(from chapter 8)

Elder Richard G. Scott said in general conference: "To ask, Why does this have to happen to me? Why do I have to suffer this, now? What have I done to cause this? will lead you into blind alleys. . . . Rather ask, What am I to do? What am I to learn from this experience? . . . How can I remember my many blessings in times of trial? Willing sacrifice of deeply held personal desires in favor of the will of God is very hard to do. Yet, when you pray with real conviction, 'Please let me know Thy will' and 'May Thy will be done,' you are in the strongest position to receive the maximum help from your loving Father" ("Trust in the Lord," *Ensign,* November 1995, 17).

President Thomas S. Monson wrote: "Yes, each of us will walk the path of disappointment. . . . Likewise shall we walk the path of pain. We cannot go to heaven in a feather bed. The Savior of the world entered after great pain and suffering. We, as servants, can expect no more than the Master. Before Easter there must be a cross" ("The Paths Jesus Walked," *Ensign,* September 1992, 4).

Watching a child go down the path of ill health that leads

from this life to the next surely must be one of the crosses spoken of by President Monson.

President Spencer W. Kimball's said: "Being human, we would expel from our lives physical pain and mental anguish and assure ourselves of continual ease and comfort, but if we were to close the doors upon sorrow and distress, we might be excluding our greatest friends and benefactors. Suffering can make saints of people as they learn patience, long-suffering, and self-mastery. The sufferings of our Savior were part of his education" (*Faith Precedes the Miracle* [Salt Lake City: Deseret Book, 1982], 98).

The Lord's timing
(from chapter 8)

Elder Neal A. Maxwell said, "Faith in God includes faith in His purposes as well as in His timing. We cannot fully accept Him while rejecting His schedule. We cannot worship Him but insist on our plans" (*That Ye May Believe* [Salt Lake City: Bookcraft, 1992], 84.

Well do I recall an event I witnessed at Primary Children's Hospital during a chapel service one Sunday morning: I was sitting behind a woman and her son, who was imprisoned in a crippled body that would not allow him to speak. At the pulpit in front of us was a man speaking of the Savior's visit to the Nephites and the wonderful miracles he performed with the children there. He referred to the experience of "babes" who were given the gift of oration. "He did loose their tongues, and they did speak . . . great and marvelous things" (3 Nephi 26:14, 16). I saw how this scripture touched the emotions of the sister in front of me. Gathering her composure, she leaned over and placed her head against the side of her son's head. Speaking through her tears, she promised her son, "Jesus will come again, and when he does, your tongue will be loosened too." Then she held her son in her arms, clearly suffering—waiting for the day. Yes, the hardest thing to have faith in is the Lord's timing.

Loved ones all around us
(from chapter 8)

This gathering of loved ones in an environment of comfort is not foreign to latter-day revelation. The Prophet Joseph Smith's words seem to refer to the kind of event my wife was experiencing: "The spirits of the just . . . are not far from us, and know and understand our thoughts, feelings, and motions, and are often pained therewith" (*Teachings of the Prophet Joseph Smith,* sel. Joseph Fielding Smith [Salt Lake City: Deseret Book, 1976], 326).

President Joseph F. Smith declared: "When messengers are sent to minister to the inhabitants of his earth, they are not strangers, but from the ranks of our kindred, friends, and fellow-beings and fellow-servants. . . . In like manner our fathers and mothers, brothers, sisters and friends who have passed away from this earth, having been faithful, and worthy to enjoy these rights and privileges, may have a mission given them to visit their relatives, and friends upon the earth again, bringing from the divine Presence messages of love, of warning, or reproof and instruction, to those whom they had learned to love in the flesh" (*Gospel Doctrine* [Salt Lake City: Deseret Book, 1975], 435–37).

He also stated in general conference: "Beyond the veil

that separates us from the spirit world, surely those who have passed beyond, can see more clearly through the veil back here to us than it is possible for us to see to them from our sphere of action. I believe we move and have our being in the presence of heavenly messengers and of heavenly beings. We are not separate from them. . . . We are closely related to our kindred, to our ancestors . . . who have preceded us into the spirit world. . . . They know us better than we know them. . . . I claim that we live in their presence, they see us, they are solicitous for our welfare, they love us now more than ever" (in Conference Reports of The Church of Jesus Christ of Latter-day Saints [Salt Lake City: The Church of Jesus Christ of Latter-day Saints, 1898 to present], April 1916, 2–3).

Elder Parley P. Pratt spoke regarding the ability of our departed loved ones to communicate with those of us here in mortality, even in dreams: "Their kindred spirits, their guardian angels, then hover about them with the fondest affection, and the most anxious solicitude. Spirit communes with spirit, thought meets thought, soul blends with soul, in all the raptures of mutual pure and eternal love. . . . In this situation we frequently hold communion with our departed father, mother, brother, sister, . . . whose affections for us . . . [are] rooted and grounded in the eternal elements" (in *Stand Ye in Holy Places* [Salt Lake City: Deseret Book, 1976], 142–43).

President Brigham Young said: "Where is the spirit world? . . . Can you see it with your natural eyes? No. Can you see spirits in this room? No. Suppose the Lord should touch your eyes that you might see, could you then see the spirits? Yes, as plainly as you now see bodies. . . . We have more friends behind the veil than on this side, and they will hail us more joyfully than you were ever welcomed by your parents and friends in this world; and you will rejoice more when you meet them than you ever rejoiced to see a friend in this life" (*Discourses of Brigham Young,* sel. John A. Widtsoe [Salt Lake City: Deseret Book, 1954], 377, 379–80).

An experience from the life of Heber J. Grant illustrates this concept of our loved ones being just beyond the veil:

> I have been blessed with only two sons. One of them died at five years of age and the other at seven. My last son died of a hip disease. . . . About an hour before he died I had a dream that his mother, who was dead, came for him, and that she brought with her a messenger, and she told this messenger to take the boy while I was asleep. In the dream I thought I awoke and I seized my son and fought for him and finally succeeded in getting him away from the messenger who had come to take him, and in so doing I dreamed that I stumbled and fell upon him.
>
> I dreamed that I fell upon his sore hip, and the terrible cries and anguish of the child drove me nearly wild. I could not stand it, and I jumped up and ran out of the house so as not to hear his distress. I dreamed that after running out of the house I met Brother Joseph E. Taylor and told him of these things.
>
> He said: "Well, Heber, do you know what I would do if my wife came for one of her children—I would not struggle for that child; I would not oppose her taking that child away. If a mother who had been faithful had passed beyond the veil, she would know of the suffering and the anguish her child may have to suffer. . . . And when you stop to think, Brother Grant, that the mother of that boy went down into the shadow of death to give him life, she is the one who ought to have the right to take him or leave him."
>
> I said, "I believe you are right, Brother Taylor, and if

she comes again, she shall have the boy without any pro-
test on my part."

After coming to that conclusion, I was waked by my
brother, B. F. Grant, who was staying that night with us.

He called me into the room and told me that my child
was dying.

I went in the front room and sat down. There was a
vacant chair between me and my wife who is now living,
and I felt the presence of that boy's deceased mother, sitting in that chair. I did not tell anybody what I felt, but I
turned to my living wife and said: "Do you feel anything
strange?" She said: "Yes, I feel assured that Heber's mother
is sitting between us, waiting to take him away."

Now, I am naturally, I believe, a sympathetic man.
. . . But I sat by the deathbed of my little boy and saw him
die, without shedding a tear. . . . I, upon that occasion
experienced a sweet, peaceful, and heavenly influence in
my home, as great as I gave ever experienced in my life.
(*Gospel Standards,* comp. G Homer Durham [Salt Lake
City: Improvement Era, 1942], 364–65)

President David O. McKay gave two examples of loved
ones from the other side of the veil waiting to welcome an
individual who was dying:

I spoke at the funeral service of a mother in Logan
only recently. That good mother, before she died, as she
lay on the bed of illness, was wont to inquire about her
brother. Nearly every night she would say, "How is he
getting along?" mentioning his name, but, suddenly, one
day that brother left his mortal existence almost instantly.
That afternoon as the sister awoke from sleep, she made
no inquiry as to the condition of her brother, didn't ask
about him, but stated, "I have seen William and Mother
together. How happy they seem. They wanted me to go

with them, but I was not ready. How happy they will be."

. . . I have seen one young man particularly responsive to that environment when he was dead to us who stood by ready to bless him, and his vocal cords could be used, for he spoke, his lips seemed to say, and distinctly I heard him say, "Yes, Father, I recognize you. May I come back?" and at the conclusion of these words his cousin, Sister Bertha Wright, said, "Administer to him Brother McKay."

I said, "It is too late, he is gone." But yet his heart was beating, his vocal cords were expressing words, but I was as conscious and sure as that I am standing here, that he was unresponsive to us. He was responding to another environment to which we were unresponsive, to which we were dead. Not five minutes passed before his heart-beat stopped, and then we said he was dead. His spirit was free, even before the heartbeat stopped. His father had been dead for fifteen years. (David O. McKay, *Gospel Ideals: Selections from the Discourses of David O. McKay*, ed. G. Homer Durham [Salt Lake City: Improvement Era, 1953], 54–55)

Little children are alive in Christ
(from chapter 9)

The Doctrine and Covenants makes this doctrine perfectly clear: "All children who die before they arrive at the years of accountability are saved in the celestial kingdom of heaven" (D&C 137:10; see also Moroni 8:8; D&C 29:46; Moses 6:54; Mosiah 15:25; JST Matthew 18:11; JST Genesis 17:11).

The Prophet Joseph Smith wrote on this subject: "All children are redeemed by the blood of Jesus Christ, and the moment that children leave this world, they are taken to the bosom of Abraham" (*History of The Church of Jesus Christ of Latter-day Saints,* ed. B. H. Roberts, 2d ed. rev., 7 vols. [Salt Lake City: The Church of Jesus Christ of Latter-day Saints, 1932–51], 4:5).

On another occasion the Prophet Joseph said, "The Lord takes many away even in infancy, that they may escape the envy of man, and the sorrows and evils of this present world; they were too pure too lovely, to live on earth; therefore, if rightly considered, instead of mourning we have reason to rejoice as they are delivered from evil, and we shall soon have them again" *(Teachings of the Prophet Joseph Smith,* sel. Joseph Fielding Smith [Salt Lake City: Deseret Book, 1976], 196–97).

Journals
(from chapter 12)

I have found the following quotations from the Brethren helpful in motivating me to keep a journal:

- "Let us then continue on in this important work of record-ing the things we do, the things we say, the things we think, to be in accordance with the instructions of the Lord. For those of you who may not have already started . . . we would suggest that this very day you begin to write your records quite fully and completely. We hope that you will do this, our brothers and sisters, for this is what the Lord has commanded" (Spencer W. Kimball, "'We Need a Listening Ear,'" *Ensign,* November 1979, 5).

- "A life that is not documented is a life that within a generation or two will largely be lost to memory. What a tragedy this can be in the history of a family. Knowledge of our ancestors shapes us and instills within us values that give direction and meaning to our lives" (Dennis B. Neuenschwander, "Bridges and Eternal Keepsakes," *Ensign,* May 1999, 84).

- "The prompting that goes unresponded to may not be repeated. Writing down what we have been prompted with is vital. A special thought can also be lost later in the day in the rough and tumble of life. God should not, and may not, choose to repeat the prompting if we assign what was given such a low priority as to put it aside" (Neal A. Maxwell, Wherefore, Ye Must Press Forward [Salt Lake City: Deseret Book, 1977], 122).

- "Some people say, 'I don't have anything to record. Nothing spiritual happens to me.' I say, 'Start recording, and spiritual things will happen. They are there all the time, but we become more sensitive to them as we write" (John H. Groberg, "Writing Your Personal and Family History," *Ensign,* May 1980, 68).

Meetings should never overshadow the needs of the individual
(from chapter 13)

Elder Thomas S. Monson shared the following story in general conference:

> Some eighty miles from Shreveport, Louisiana, lives the Jack Methvin family. . . . Until just recently there was a lovely daughter who, by her presence, graced that home. Her name was Christal. She was but ten years old when death ended her earthly sojourn. . . .
>
> Her future was bright, and life was wonderful. Then

there was discovered on her leg an unusual lump. The specialists in New Orleans completed their diagnosis and rendered their verdict: Carcinoma. The leg must be removed.

She recovered well from the surgery, lived as buoyantly as ever and never complained. Then the doctors discovered that the cancer had spread to her tiny lungs. The Methvin family did not despair, but rather planned a flight to Salt Lake City. Christal could receive a blessing from one of the General Authorities. The Methvins knew none of the Brethren personally, so opening before Christal a picture of all the General Authorities, a chance selection was made. By sheer coincidence, my name was selected.

Christal never made the flight to Salt Lake City. Her condition deteriorated. The end drew nigh. But her faith did not waver. To her parents, she said, "Isn't stake conference approaching? Isn't a General Authority assigned? And why not Brother Monson? If I can't go to him, the Lord can send him to me."

Meanwhile in Salt Lake City, with no knowledge of the events transpiring in Shreveport, a most unusual situation developed. For the weekend of the Shreveport Louisiana Stake Conference, I had been assigned to El Paso, Texas. President Ezra Taft Benson called me to his office and explained that one of the other Brethren had done some preparatory work regarding the stake division in El Paso. He asked if I would mind were another to be assigned to El Paso and I assigned elsewhere. Of course there was no problem—anywhere would be fine with me. Then President Benson said, "Brother Monson, I feel impressed to have you visit the Shreveport Louisiana Stake." The assignment was accepted. The day came. I arrived in Shreveport.

That Saturday afternoon was filled with meetings. . . . Rather apologetically, Stake President Charles F. Cagle asked if my schedule would permit me time to provide a blessing to a ten-year-old girl afflicted with cancer. . . . Knowing the time was tightly scheduled, President Cagle almost whispered that Christal was confined to her home—*more than eighty miles from Shreveport!*

I examined the schedule of meetings for that evening and the next morning. . . . There simply was no available time. An alternative suggestion came to mind. Could we not remember the little one in our public prayers at conference? Surely the Lord would understand. On this basis, we proceeded with the scheduled meetings.

When the word was communicated to the Methvin family, there was understanding but a trace of disappointment as well. . . . Again the family prayed, asking for a final favor—that their precious Christal would realize her desire.

At the very moment the Methvin family knelt in prayer, the clock in the stake center showed the time to be 1:45. . . . I was sorting my notes, preparing to step to the pulpit, when I heard a voice speak to my spirit. The message was brief, the words familiar: "Suffer the little children to come unto me, and forbid them not: for of such is the kingdom of God" (Mark 10:14). My notes became a blur. My thoughts turned to a tiny girl in need of a blessing. . . . The meeting schedule was altered. After all, *people are more important than meetings.* . . .

The Methvin family had just arisen from their knees when the telephone rang and the message was relayed that early Sunday morning . . . we would journey to Christal's bedside.

I shall ever remember and never forget that early-morning journey to a heaven the Methvin family calls home. . . . The family surrounded Christal's bedside. I gazed down at a child who was too ill to rise—almost too weak to speak. Her illness had now rendered her sightless. So strong was the spirit that I fell to my knees, took her frail hand in mine, and said simply, "Christal, I am here."

She parted her lips and whispered, "Brother Monson, I just knew you would come." I looked around the room. No one was standing. Each was on bended knee. A blessing was given. A faint smile crossed Christal's face. Her whispered "thank you" provided an appropriate benediction. . . . The pure spirit of Christal Methvin left its disease-ravaged body and entered the paradise of God. ("The Faith of a Child," *Ensign,* November 1975, 20–22; emphasis added)

The proper spiritual pace must include the proper priority of one-on-one service; otherwise, our activity in the Church may unknowingly become little more than a clutter of meetings diminishing our ability to reach beyond the chapel. Fortunately, for Christal and the Methvin family, Elder Monson understood that there is an appropriate time for planning meetings, and there is a time when meetings are not appropriate.

Serving for the right reasons
(from chapter 14)

Elder Dallin H. Oaks wrote of the six reasons that people serve in the Church:

People serve one another for different reasons. . . . [1] Some serve for hope of earthly reward. Such a man or woman may serve in a Church position or in private acts of mercy in an effort to achieve prominence or cultivate contacts that will increase income or aid in acquiring wealth. Others may serve in order to obtain worldly honors, prominence, or power. . . . The scriptural word for gospel service "for the sake of riches and honor" is *priestcraft* (Alma 1:16). . . . [2] Another reason for service . . . is that which is motivated by a desire to obtain good companionship. We surely have good associations in our

Church service, but is that an acceptable motive for service? . . . Persons who serve only to obtain good companionship are more selective in choosing their friends than the Master was in choosing his servants. [3] Some serve out of fear of punishment. The scriptures abound with descriptions of the miserable state of those who fail to follow the commandments of God. . . . [4] Other persons serve out of a sense of duty or out of loyalty to family, friends, or traditions. I would call such persons "good soldiers." They instinctively do what they are asked, without question. . . . Such persons . . . do much good. We have all benefited from their good works. . . . Service of this character is worthy of praise and will surely qualify for blessings, especially if it is done willingly and joyfully. . . . [5] One such higher reason for service is the hope of an eternal reward. This hope . . . is one of our most powerful motivations. . . .

The above five motives for service have a common deficiency. In varying degrees each focuses on the actor's personal advantage, either on earth or in the judgment to follow. Each is self-centered. There is something deficient about any service that is conscious of self. A few months after my calling to the Council of the Twelve, I expressed my feelings of inadequacy to one of the senior members of my quorum. He responded with this mild reproof and challenging insight: "I suppose your feelings are understandable. But you should work for a condition where you will not be preoccupied with yourself and your own feelings and can give your entire concern to others, to the work of the Lord in all the world." Those who seek to follow [the Savior's] . . . example must lose themselves in their service to others. . . . [6] If our service is to be most efficacious, it must be unconcerned with self and heedless of personal advantage. It must be accomplished for the love of God and the love of his children. . . . Here we learn that it is not enough to serve God with all of our *might* and *strength*. He who looks into our hearts and knows our minds demands more than this. In order to stand blameless before God at the last day, we must also serve him with all our *heart* and *mind*. (*Pure in Heart* [Salt Lake City: Bookcraft, 1988], 38–49)